Happy Mother's Day 1995

Lo

D1008216

Daughters

WOMEN OF
THE BIBLE
SPEAK TO
WOMEN
OF TODAY

of Eve

VIRGINIA STEM OWENS

NAVPRESS ◢
BRINGING TRUTH TO LIFE
NavPress Publishing Group
P.O. Box 35001, Colorado Springs, Colorado 80935

The Navigators is an international Christian organization. Jesus Christ gave His followers the Great Commission to go and make disciples (Matthew 28:19). The aim of The Navigators is to help fulfill that commission by multiplying laborers for Christ in every nation.

NavPress is the publishing ministry of The Navigators. NavPress publications are tools to help Christians grow. Although publications alone cannot make disciples or change lives, they can help believers learn biblical discipleship, and apply what they learn to their lives and ministries.

Library of Congress Catalog Card Number:
94-38148
ISBN 08910-98240

Cover illustration: Cindy Lindgren

Scripture quotations in this publication are taken from the HOLY BIBLE: NEW INTERNATIONAL VERSION® (NIV®), Copyright © 1973, 1978, 1984 by International Bible Society, used by permission of Zondervan Publishing House, all rights reserved; and the King James Version (KJV).

ISBN 0-89109-824-0

Printed in the United States of America

Published in association with the literary agency of
Alive Communications, P.O. Box 49068,
Colorado Springs, CO 80949.

CONTENTS

AUTHOR'S NOTE

So plainly is this not a work of scholarship that I hardly need to disavow such an intention. I have accepted the stories whole, as they stand in the received text, rather than investigating their origin, which as with all stories, is ultimately irrecoverable and past our finding out.

I have often paraphrased the characters' dialogue in a more contemporary idiom. Nevertheless, I have remained true to the actual text. Biblical narrative is always sparing in its details. Large gaps of time may be passed over with a single word or phrase, sometimes with no time indicator at all. Characters' motives are rarely spelled out. Instead, the narrative leaves space for the reader to speculate. I have tried to indicate when my descriptions of a character's thoughts or actions come from my own reflection on the text by introducing them with terms such as "possibly," "maybe," etc.

AUTHOR

Virginia Stem Owens has published eight non-fiction books on subjects ranging from the counterculture of the 1960s to the church's use of media to contemporary physics. Her latest works are a trilogy of suspense novels set in East Texas— *At Point Blank, Congregation*, and *A Multitude of Sins*.

Born in Houston, she spent part of her childhood in Huntsville, Texas, and graduated from North Texas University. She has graduate degrees from Kansas University (literature) and the Iliff School of Theology in Denver. She has taught at Texas A&M University, Friends University in Wichita, Kansas, and is currently Director of The Milton Center, an institute for writers of Christian faith based at Kansas Newman College in Wichita.

A contributing editor to the journal *Perspectives*, she has published in a wide variety of periodicals, including *Mother Earth News, Christianity Today, The Dallas Morning News, The Houston Chronicle, Kalos: Arte y Cultura* (Barcelona), and *Media Development* (London).

The Texas Institute of Letters awarded her book *If You Do Love Old Men* the Carr P. Collins Award for best non-fiction work in 1990.

She and her husband live in Wichita during the academic year, returning to their home in Huntsville for the summer.

Introduction
WOMEN'S WAYS:
WOMEN OF THE BIBLE
SPEAK TO WOMEN OF TODAY

*I*t was my mother who first introduced me to biblical women. For the most part, this was a thinly disguised attempt on her part to socialize my often unsociable nature. She used Hannah, the mother of Samuel, to impress upon me, a child who didn't even like to play dolls, how important children are to women and how important I was to her. Unfortunately, however, the story had the opposite of its intended effect. I was horrified that a mother would abandon her child at the tender age of three to an aging clergyman, a kind of priestly Rumpelstiltskin. Next she tried the story of Miriam, emphasizing her obedience and resourcefulness as a baby-sitter for the infant Moses hidden in the bulrushes. The message was pretty clear. If Miriam could save her little brother from Pharaoh's cruel soldiers, the least I could do was keep mine from running out in the street.

That was fifty years ago.

In the past few decades we've come to realize our distance from those women. The details of their world—drawing water at the town well, herding sheep, arranged marriages based primarily on economics, worth gauged by childbearing—all make their lives seem not only ancient but alien to us. Can those women have anything significant to tell us today?

Of course, certain basic attributes of human nature remain the same over time. People are still envious like Cain, fearful like Isaac, arrogant like Saul, hopeful like Anna. And their words from the ancient world still speak to our condition. At least when we consider ourselves generically as human beings.

But is there any special word to women found in the lives of scriptural women? Is there any gender-specific wisdom to be gleaned from these stories?

After all, women are no longer considered property. Instead, they vote, hold office, own property, marry and divorce as they choose, decide when or if to have children, obtain whatever education their society provides, determine their own careers. Widows don't have to rely, as Tamar did, on the levirate marriage law—the obligation of a man to marry his brother's widow. A woman "taken in adultery" is unlikely to lose her life or even her reputation. An infertile couple, unlike Hannah and Elkanah, have any number of medical options open to them—sperm banks, in vitro fertilization, even surrogate uterus agreements. And such a mother would never give her child away. If she did, she'd find herself entangled in legal snares—as would any father who, like Jephthah, proposed to slaughter his daughter to fulfill an ill-considered vow. Those things just don't happen in the modern world.

Or do they?

How much has life really changed for women? Are there, in fact, gendered propensities that persist over time, threads that run through time and across cultures revealing essential patterns? Are we, even after centuries of change, still "sisters under the skin" with the Middle Eastern, North African, and Mediterranean women who people the biblical pages? Do their fears and sorrows, hopes and joys connect with ours? If we paid attention to them—not as cultural oddities or bit players in the biblical drama—would they have anything significant to say to us?

One way to tell is to look. Over 150 women are named in the Bible. How many of these do we know? Most of us have trouble naming a dozen. Though the writers and compilers of Scripture have taken a lot of heat recently as patriarchal chauvinists, they included more women in the story than we have paid attention to. Puritans used to give their daughters names like Hephzibah and Jemima because they knew who those biblical women were.

We don't. And if we don't know their names, much less their stories, how can we hope to glean any insight those stories might offer? Most biblical commentaries, I find, seem blind to the part women play in scriptural stories. Thus they systematically, if unconsciously, exclude these characters from exegetical consideration.

I decided to sift the pages of Scripture for these women. What follows is their stories. Some you may know; others will be less familiar. Don't expect them all to be admirable characters. Just like their male counterparts, the women of the Bible can be malicious, stupid, vengeful, and conniving. But the *ways* in which they are courageous or cowardly, devoted or deceitful are, I believe, peculiarly women's ways, colored by the exigencies of gender. I have arranged these stories in groups according to issues women find urgent today—issues like rape and multiple marriages. And, strange though it seems, and as much as cultures have changed in the intervening millennia, I have found plenty of stories to fill the categories.

Back to my mother, where I began. She was born the same year the Nineteenth Amendment to the Constitution granted women the right to vote. Yet few of my own friends and acquaintances, despite their greater opportunities, know much about Hannah or Miriam. Many of these friends and acquaintances are what we now call "professional women"—a term I used to find irritating. The term indicates someone who has studied and trained for a vocation, not a gender. Teachers, lawyers, doctors. Professional athletes, maybe, or professional musicians. But professional *women?*

Then I think of my mother. She, like most of us, has found being a woman a difficult undertaking. While there are no bar exams, no certifications, no degrees, she has studied for this vocation all her life. What she has studied has been Scripture. And the part she's found most illuminating, most tenable, are not the overtly instructive portions about covering your head or keeping quiet, but the stories. And not only Hannah's and Miriam's. She can scheme like Rebekah, be as adamant as the Syro-Phoenician woman, and should the need arise, I have no doubt she could drive a stake through a man's head like Jael.

My mother would never call herself a courageous person, and certainly not a daring one. But there have been many occasions on which she was called upon to act with nobility. She knows how to do this too. Where did she learn it? Whom did she use as a model? I believe it was the vassal queen for whom she is named. Esther.

Mothers

I start my examination of the Bible's women where we all, male or female, begin—with mothers. Though the ancient world—just as our own—produced bad mothers as well as good ones, changing social patterns have probably affected motherhood less than any other human bond, including marriage. The mother-child relationship has endured millennia of pushing and pulling with very little alteration to its essential character.

Whether women can take any particular credit for this could be debated. Do mothers, in whatever culture, continue to nurture and sacrifice for their children because women possess superior, more magnanimous natures, or is their mothering merely biologically based instinct? Whatever the answer to that question, whether the cause is genetic programming, cultural conditioning, or conscious choice, the fact is that women routinely attend to and care for their offspring more than men, a state of affairs that has persisted for millennia.

Its persistence, however, does not always guarantee that maternal nurturing actually benefits the child. Samson's mother, known only to us as the wife of Manoah, went to great lengths to raise her boy by all the rules prescribed by the angel who announced her impending pregnancy. Yet all her watchful care did not keep her son from falling into the hands of the designing Delilah.

Maternity then, though frequently portrayed as steadfast and selfless in the Bible, is not presented as an absolute or ultimate value. And just as well for women, simply because

11

not all women are mothers. The Bible does not value women solely, or even primarily, for their ability to reproduce. Otherwise, we could make nothing of women like Deborah and Esther from the Old Testament or a whole raft of New Testament women, including Anna the prophetess, Mary Magdalene, Mary and Martha of Bethany, Dorcas, Lydia, Joanna, Susanna, and Priscilla.

Nevertheless, we begin with mothers since they do embody that bond among our species that has endured virtually unchanged over centuries and with whom we can thus most easily connect.

EVE: THE FIRST MOTHER

Genesis 1:26-31, 2:18–4:26

With the possible exception of Mary, Eve is the most misunderstood woman of the Bible. She has been wrenched from the actual words of the text, then shoved and pounded into various shapes to fit whatever void a culture feels in its collective psyche. So many alterations has she undergone, so many cultural reconstructions has she suffered, so many private purposes has she served, that it is next to impossible to get past this most symbolic of all females to examine the "real" woman.

Most people's image of Eve owes more to Milton's *Paradise Lost* than to Genesis. From Saint Paul to C. S. Lewis, writers have used her to make theological points about human nature. This was inevitable, of course. The same thing happened to Adam. Being the first of one's kind, a prototype, inevitably bestows unusual significance. We expect that essential information about ourselves is wrapped up in this original pair; they contain the secret to ourselves. And, according to which theologian one reads, Eve's story is proof of women's inferior reason, their innate feminine guile, or

13

their superior daring and courage.

Let's start with the story itself then, in the hope of coming closer to the original and thus seeing more clearly.

In the first chapter of Genesis, God produces the human race generically and in his own image—"male and female created he them"[1]—a fact repeated verbatim in the fifth chapter. There, both male and female are called "Adam."[2] Strictly speaking, neither of the pair becomes an actor in this drama until the second chapter when they are provided with a setting, "a garden eastward in Eden."[3] Eve doesn't receive a separate name until late in the third chapter—after the pair's expulsion from the garden.

But we're getting ahead of ourselves. First, we are presented with the solitary figure we know as Adam but whose name, to get the full effect in English, should be called something like Earthly, since the name in Hebrew means "of the ground." While plentifully supplied with food, pleasant scenery, and stimulating projects (tending the garden and naming the animals), Earthly is nevertheless lonely. He can't find a suitable companion amongst the entire menagerie God presents him with. He can name them, but they can't return the favor.

Specifically to remedy this, God performs a primal act of genetic engineering, producing from Earthly's own flesh and bone a companion. Recognizing this new creature to be of the same genus as himself, yet curiously different, he gives her a name that reflects this, calling her Woman. (The effect of the added syllable in English is similar to the Hebrew: Man = *Ish;* Woman = *Ishah.*)

Since there's only the two of them, they feel no need to bother with clothes, which hadn't been invented yet anyway. They are both rare, indeed unique; they have no one else to compare themselves or one another to and thus no shame.

Enter the serpent.

He speaks to Woman.

The rest, as we say, is history.

Much has been made of those six short verses containing

the interchange between Woman and the serpent and its result. Some theologians have claimed that the serpent approached the woman because her weaker mental and spiritual powers made her more susceptible to temptation. Others maintain that, on the contrary, her more active intelligence led her to experiment with the tree of knowledge. One thing is certain: Everything we know as human civilization, from manufacturing ("they sewed fig leaves together, and made themselves aprons"[4]) to psychology ("the eyes of them both were opened, and they knew that they were naked"[5]) came from her experiment. From wisdom to war, it's all there, wrapped up in that one inquisitive mouthful.

During the fateful encounter, Earthly himself remains oddly passive, never opening his mouth except to take the bite the woman offers him. We're not even sure where he is during the critical conversation between the woman and the serpent. Later, when Earthly is called on to answer for his own disobedience, he points an accusing finger at his companion. Ironic, especially since ever afterward men would consider themselves bolder and more fearless than women.

But then, lots of things changed after that; the world didn't make sense the way it had before. It didn't operate with its previous harmony of purposes. Woman's independence suddenly comes to an end when she chooses to imitate Earthly's response to the divine interrogation. He blames her for the disaster; she loses her originality by following his example and blaming the serpent. The serpent itself crawls off—now just a mute snake in the grass. The end of cross-species conversations.

Even the weather changed. The mists that had gently watered the garden were replaced by storm and drought. Weeds supplanted parsley. The world turned carnivorous. In fact, God himself, realizing fig-leaf aprons wouldn't hold up to the wear and tear of farming, replaced their vegetarian clothing with animal-skin coats. Creation kept on operating, but the basis of its economy was no longer so benign. The unhappy couple are evicted from their home. Earthly had to go to work.

But with all the loss, Woman also got something—a name. At that point in their depleted circumstances, it was about all that Earthly could afford to give her. He called her Eve. Or, strictly speaking in English, Living.

And earthly living, as every generation since has known it, began.

First thing off the bat, of course, Living gets pregnant. Second thing off the bat she gets pregnant again. The Lord God hadn't been kidding when he said he would greatly multiply her conception. And her sorrow. The curse he laid on her ("thy desire shall be to thy husband, and he shall rule over thee"[6]) resulted in just that—conception and sorrow. Men, having on average 30 percent more body weight, have dominated women physically ever since. But women have also been driven by their own irrational desire, with the erotic impulse inevitably yielding to the maternal function.

"The mother of all living"[7] she's called in Genesis. And every ancient civilization we know anything about, from the Sumerians on, preserved some version of this blank-faced Mother-of-All-Living. Some of the oldest artifacts known to the human race are images of her. Small limestone or ivory figures with bulbous breasts and hips dating from as far back as the Ice Age have been found all over the world, their faces always smooth and featureless. A stylized female figure carved from mammoth ivory, found near Pekarna, Czechoslovakia, has a hole where the face should be.

Her identity absorbed by her maternal function, Eve remains essentially invisible to her progeny, the whole human race. Coming directly from God's fashioning hand, she had been unique, possessed of personhood. But a prototype, by its very nature, has no individuality. Once she became the Mother-of-All-Living, that individuality was submerged in the enormity of her mythic proportions. Such immense figures, looming larger than Mount Rushmore in our vision, look featureless. And mothers ever after have shared Living's fate.

In their children's eyes, they have no name. They are always "Mama," "Mom," "Mother."

Now this is a state of affairs that women, for the most part, accept with joy. Your toddler stretches yearning little arms toward you, and you melt. Your Cub Scout snuggles against your side, and your very bones begin to glow.

God had no doubt felt the same way about Earthly and Living in the garden—full of tenderness, eager to answer every need. And, like him, every mother of a teenager knows what it feels like suddenly, overnight, to be perceived as "the enemy" by these darlings on whom we have lavished such care. It is then that we learn how much of a catastrophe the Fall was, not just for the human race, but for God; how he must have suffered from "empty-nest syndrome" when he sent those original children forth to make their own way in the world. And how brave he was to let them go. In motherhood we come as close as any human can to both the joy and agony of God himself.

Conceiving and grieving—that was Eve's lot in post-garden life. Note the lack of softness or sentimentality in this picture of the first maternity. Pain and sorrow are its identifying marks, not pink and blue layettes. The first child born into this world, Living's firstborn, murders his younger brother. The Mother-of-All-Living is also the Mother-of-Killing.

We must mention here a rather spooky correlation in the ancient world to this part of the story. The Mother-of-All-Living goddess, known in Canaan as Astarte, was universally worshiped around the Middle East. Her temples contained "asherah," stone or wood poles that, like the faceless figurines mentioned earlier, represented her fertile presence in the land. The Bible mentions these worship sites in a number of places, most frequently to warn against them. For one thing, women of all classes hired themselves out as prostitutes there to insure their fertility. These temples were often bloody places. On their altars were sacrificed not only animals, but at times of particular social stress, human children.

The Mother-of-All-Living becoming the Mother-of-Killing—an ultimate perversion of what we call today maternal instinct.

Eve had to endure one son's murder and the other's guilt. In her sorrow, we finally see Woman become a woman. Her suffering makes her an individual to us. Turning her into a goddess can only diminish her reality. Evading her humanity and claiming her divinity leads to degradation of her sex and death for her children.

We have only one more glimpse of poor Living. Bereaved of one son, without hope of ever seeing again the one who's been exiled, she is giving birth to yet a third son. This one she names Seth—"Compensation." And birth-racked, death-racked Eve finally seems human.

SARAH

Genesis 11:17–12:20, 16:1–18:15, 20:1–21:21, 23:1-2

or a long time after Eve, women were mentioned in the Bible for no other attribute than their ability to bear children. Even the "daughters of men,"[1] beautiful enough to attract the attention of the mysterious "sons of God"[2] in the sixth chapter of Genesis, are only noted because their offspring became "men of renown."[3] In the genealogies of this period, only sons are named; bloodlines were traced through named fathers, not the unnamed mothers. Only three women between Eve and Sarah are identified by name—Adah, Zillah, and Zillah's daughter Naamah—and then only because of their sons' and brother's accomplishments.

Following this long string of nameless women, we come upon Sarah—or Sarai as she was originally called—and finally we have a character with definition and distinct outlines, one equal in interest to her husband Abram.

On God's command the couple had set out, along with their nephew Lot, from Haran, then a city in what is now southern Turkey. Though already past her prime, Sarai is still

sufficiently well-preserved to attract the pharaoh's attention during a stopover in Egypt. Since they had gone there
seeking relief from one of the Middle East's periodic famines,
Abram is afraid to deny his host's appetite and so instructs
Sarai to assent to the imperial advances. Pleased with Abram's
agreement, Pharaoh sends him a generous dowry of livestock
and slaves.

Is Sarai herself a willing accomplice to this fraud? Her
reaction isn't recorded. We do know, however, that she doesn't
give the game away. It's God, in fact, who intervenes to save
her. Pharaoh's household is immediately beset by plague. Sensing cosmic displeasure, he uncovers the deception and returns
Sarai to her husband, protesting Abram's abuse of his hospitality.

Assessing the moral weight of this episode requires a delicate set of scales. The people who originally preserved this
story would not necessarily have seen this incident in the same
light we do. We are offended not only by Abram's outright lie,
but even more by his willingness to use his wife's body to save
his own skin. When he actually makes a profit on the deal,
Abram sinks in our estimation to the level of a pimp.

Yet ethical behavior is not the point of the story. Destiny is. In this case, Sarai's. God intervenes, not because of
moral issues, but because Pharaoh's harem wasn't what he had
planned for her. She was destined for the founding of nations,
as essential to that equation as Abram.

Although Sarai's complicity in the pharaoh scam remains
unclear at this point, the next episode shows her hatching a
plot of her own.

Years pass. The couple grows older and, supposedly, less
fertile. Prospects for the promised child grow dimmer. The
entourage wanders around the Negev, wealthy nomads always
on uneasy terms with the settled people whose land they
haunt. From time to time Abram receives divine reassurances
that his descendants will indeed be as many as the stars in
the sky. Meanwhile, the cradle remains empty.

Then Sarai gets an idea. She chooses Hagar, a slave woman acquired in Egypt—possibly part of Pharaoh's gift package—as her reproductive proxy. Surrogate motherhood was in fact an established practice in that part of the world, employed most often, just as today, by upscale, infertile women who could afford the considerable costs involved. Abram, true to form, offers no more protest to his wife's plan than Adam had to Eve's picnic in paradise.

And the outcome, once more, is catastrophic.

Instead of rejoicing at the success of her plan when Hagar conceives, Sarai complains to her husband that Hagar is getting uppity. "You're responsible for what I'm having to put up with now," she tells him, shifting the blame for her ill-considered scheme onto his shoulders. "I gave her permission to sleep with you, and now that she turns up pregnant, she thinks she's more of a woman than I am. God knows this is your fault, not mine."

Once again Abram shows himself to be hardly hero material. "Do what you want. It's up to you," he says, abandoning the woman carrying his child to the fury of her jealous rival. Thus encouraged, Sarai makes the pregnant Hagar's life so miserable that the woman runs away temporarily, ready to take her chances in the desert rather than submit to her abusive mistress.

After Sarai's scheme fails, there seems to be nothing more the pair can do but wait. For thirteen more years. At last God speaks to Abram again. This time, to signal a new start, he changes both the couple's names. Abram becomes Abraham, "father of many nations."[4] Sarai becomes Sarah, the feminine form of "ruler" or "prince." Along with the new names, the Lord renews his promise to give the pair a son.

This is one too many for Abraham, however. Overcome by the absurdity of fathering a child at ninety-nine, to say nothing of his wife conceiving at ninety, he literally falls down laughing. When he recovers, he suggests a more reasonable alternative. Why not use Ishmael, the son Hagar has already provided, as the pipeline for this population explosion? But God continues to insist that Sarah will also bear a son. As if to seal the deal, he even provides the name for this elusive infant—Isaac. "Laughter."

Not long afterward, three strangers show up at Abraham's encampment near the Mamre oasis. He offers them the customary hospitality of the desert, hurrying off to enlist Sarah's aid. As the three strangers are eating *alfresco* the meal prepared in their honor, one of them asks Abraham where his wife is. Satisfied that she is inside the tent (and therefore within hearing range), this Stranger predicts that before another year is out she'll have a new baby.

Eavesdropping on the conversation, Sarah is suddenly overcome by the postmenopausal irony. Maybe she'd been luscious enough to tempt a king twenty-five years ago, but she knows she's now as shriveled and juiceless as her spineless husband. Her crone's cackle can be heard from inside the tent.

The prophetic Stranger, however, is not amused. In one of the most delicate scenes in this whole saga, he speaks directly to Sarah, demanding to know just what she finds so funny. Suddenly fearful, she denies her splutter of mirth. The Stranger, however, remains curiously adamant. "Oh," he insists, "but you *did* laugh."

Between this point in the story and the actual arrival of the long-promised child, two other episodes, at first glance unrelated, are interjected. First, the sad tale of Sodom and Gomorrah, in which Lot's wife turns to a pillar of salt when she looks back at the flames consuming her former home. Perhaps she appears as a contrast to Sarah who, despite her other failings, never looked back but trekked up and down Mesopotamia with Abraham for the better part of a century.

Second, Lot's daughters, having fled the cities with their father, are living in a cave in the mountains—not a likely spot for meeting eligible bachelors. Fearing they will end up old maids, they conspire to get their father drunk and themselves pregnant. And they succeed. The episode ends with an amazingly low-key acknowledgment that the Moabite and Ammonite peoples were the products of this incest. The Israelites would have had no trouble catching the implication, however. The scheme of Lot's daughters parallels Sarah's own rash act of giving Hagar to Abram to assure offspring for the couple. Hagar's son Ishmael, along with Moab and Ammon, became the ancestors of Israel's persistent enemies.

A third episode that interrupts the progress of the story toward Sarah's motherhood appears at first glance to be a replay of her encounter with the Egyptian pharaoh, only this time Abraham offers his wife to Abimelech, the king of Gerar.

On closer examination, a significant difference in the episodes emerges, however. Unlike the pharaoh, Abimelech is not smitten with Sarah's beauty, now long-faded. In fact, Abraham doesn't even wait for Abimelech to make the first move. He foists off Sarah as his sister before the king even asks.

After Abimelech takes her (how enthusiastically is not clear), God warns the king in a dream that he has been duped by his guests and should return Sarah to her husband. Horrified, Abimelech protests that he merely took Abraham's word that the woman was his sister, adding that Sarah herself had gone along with the deal.

The next day, when the king demands that Abraham explain his behavior, he uses the same defense as before—his fear. He even tries to mitigate his deception by protesting that Sarah is in fact his half sister. Furthermore, he adds that the two of them had cooked up this scheme long ago, before they left Haran.

Abimelech is the only one who comes off looking good in this sordid little incident. He restores Sarah and gives Abraham and his entourage permission to camp anywhere in his kingdom. Also he tells Sarah he's paid off her "brother" to the tune of a thousand silver shekels—the usual price for a public certificate of chastity. Considering her diminished appeal, the gesture was itself something of a joke.

Such a formality might have been a necessary precaution,

however. Sarah would certainly not have wanted anyone snickering over who Isaac's father was—Abimelech or Abraham— when the promised child arrives not many months afterward. Thus the two old con artists do finally get what they've waited for so long—the boy called Laughter. But by now his name echoes with many meanings.

Consider, for example, Sarah's burst of unusually long dialogue at her son's birth. She exclaims, "God has made laughter for me; everyone who hears will laugh over me. Who would have said to Abraham that Sarah would suckle children? Yet I have borne him a son in his old age."[5]

What are we to make of this play on Isaac's name in these postpartum remarks? At whom are they directed? What is their tone? Is Sarah simply inviting those around her to rejoice with her over the birth? Or do we detect a note of thin-skinned waspishness? Does she suspect that people are ridiculing rather than rejoicing? Is Sarah laughing at her own improbable situation, a mother at ninety, the ludicrous butt of history's longest practical joke? Certainly there's a bit of nose-thumbing in the remark about Abraham. But to whom is the taunt directed—her mockers or her husband? Whatever Sarah's meaning, she appears to have forgotten that she had laughed at the Stranger's prophecy herself. And certainly her final comment is tinged with spiteful pride. Unfortunately, it foreshadows Sarah's final scene.

We would prefer for her story to end here. Then, despite our qualms about Sarah's earlier conduct, we might find some consolation in our last glimpse of her as an aged madonna, enjoying her long-awaited maternal fulfillment. But there's one last episode to recount. And it's not a pretty picture.

Hagar still lives in Abraham's camp with her son Ishmael, now a young teenager. The pair continue to be, however, the fly in Sarah's ointment. So she goes to Abraham to demand that the slave woman be driven from the camp again, along with her son. She tells her husband she fears that, after he dies, Ishmael will inherit equally with her own son, Isaac.

To his credit, Abraham is greatly distressed at the thought of losing his firstborn son. For once he even shows some backbone and resists his wife's demands. God, however, knowing Sarah's capacity for cruelty even better than her husband, instructs Abraham to acquiesce, promising both protection and proliferation for Ishmael, just as he has for Isaac. The next morning, after loading Hagar with provisions, Abraham watches the woman and his firstborn son head off into the desert alone.

Was Sarah watching from inside the tent again? Did she laugh this time too?

Nothing more is ever said of Sarah, except that she lived another twenty-seven years, dying in the land of Canaan, still a nomad. She is not mentioned in the story of Abraham taking Isaac to Mount Moriah to sacrifice him. I doubt her husband dared tell her.

When she died, Abraham, her old partner in crime, grieved for her and spent a considerable sum, four hundred silver shekels (leftover from Abimelech's payoff?), to buy a field to bury her in near Mamre, the place where she had once laughed at the Stranger.

How has Sarah fared in later treatments of her? Despite her less than admirable history, both Jewish and Christian tradition have habitually elevated Sarah to epic eminence. The author of the letter to the Hebrews, ignoring her less savory characteristics, places her among the heroes of faith. But instead of Sarah the Faithful, she could as easily be called Sarah the Scornful or Sarah the Spiteful. Even Sarah the Seductress. But Sarah the Saintly? Sarah the Model of Meek Motherhood? Hardly.

It's not as though I'm slanting the facts of Sarah's story or giving those facts an outlandish interpretation. Read her story for yourself. She was, as we say, all too real, all too human. But if you're interested in the reality of women's lives, you can't ignore her, for just as Eve shows us the sorrow of motherhood, Sarah shows us its ferocity. Though she had the morality of a gun moll, she clung tenaciously to the promise of motherhood. I've even considered the possibility that, suspecting Abraham of sterility, she agreed to pass herself off as his sister, hoping for better luck with Pharaoh or Abimelech. When she tried another ploy and set up Hagar as a surrogate, she discovered that another woman's child could not satisfy her consuming desire for one of her own. Her lamentable rage against Hagar was in direct proportion to the frustration of her maternal hopes.

I could, I suppose, compare Sarah's hot pursuit of pregnancy with the more antiseptic, technological methods practiced by women today—in vitro fertilization, rent-a-womb plans, sperm banks. That's a discussion that needs to happen, though I don't intend to attempt it here. At least not directly.

Biology, Freud said, is destiny. And women both ancient and modern have always been aware of how much their lives are determined by the biochemical sea, washing their internal shores. But Sarah was more than a biological clock running down, a virago made frantic by infertility. She knew that destiny means more than biology; it is also history. She realized that the birth of a child is not merely the end product of a biological process but an historical event. She yearned for Isaac, not simply to satisfy biological needs but as a fulfillment of promise, a promise that fueled the future. And every mother, setting her toddler on its feet, sees history stumbling forward in those unsteady steps.

Motherhood is one of the world's fiercest occupations, and Sarah was one of its fiercest practitioners. For good reason is it stoked and fired by elemental hormones, driving women against whatever odds not merely to reproduce but to nourish and protect offspring. Because it's not just the survival of the species that's at stake, but the history of the world.

MARY

Matthew 1:18–2:23; Mark 3:21-22,31-34; Luke 1:26–2:20;
John 2:1-11; 19:25-27

*M*ary's first appearance in Scripture is a love scene, not a theological treatise. A young girl in the small country town of Nazareth, full of life and health, is anticipating her coming marriage to Joseph, about whom we know little except that he is once called a carpenter. Mary's fiancé, from the picture Matthew gives us, might well have been an older man, seasoned by experience so that he handles difficulties with equanimity. Whether or not Mary was romantically smitten with him, her family probably considered him something of a catch.

At any rate, Mary is alone, possibly daydreaming about the approaching wedding, when she is startled by the sudden arrival of a strange visitor. Did the angel Gabriel appear in a blinding light, beating wings that spanned the room? Probably not, since Luke says the girl was troubled by the angel Gabriel's words, not his appearance. He begins by paying her outrageous compliments: she is "full of grace," he tells her, favored by God, the lucky winner in a sweepstakes she didn't even know she'd entered. No mere mortal in all the Scriptures is ever addressed in such lofty terms. Mary, whose mother had no doubt taught her to beware of flattering words from strange men, "cast in her mind what manner of salutation this should be."[1]

The stranger's next words are even more fantastic, however. Most men bent on seduction would have assured her she had nothing to worry about. This one, on the other hand, predicts she will in fact get pregnant, that the baby will be a boy, and that she should name him Jesus—a common enough name in that day, something like Victor in English. Only this time the content of the name is to be taken seriously. The child really will be victorious, indeed a king, destined to restore her country's throne to its rightful owner.

Well, Mary may be young, but she's not stupid. She brushes aside the stranger's apparent flattery and glittering promises about the future and pulls the conversation firmly back to the present. "Just how do you expect me to believe all that?" she demands. "I'm not even married yet. And I'm not the kind of girl who fools around." The implication is that she doesn't intend to become one either. Having protected her valuable virginity so far, she's not about to jeopardize it now for some stranger's wild promises.

Gabriel is forced at this point to reveal the principal for whom he's acting: not he, but God himself will be her Lover. And, as if recognizing how incredible this explanation sounds, he offers as proof of his promises the news that Mary's elderly cousin Elizabeth, childless throughout a long marriage, is now miraculously six months pregnant herself.

Faced with the stranger's possession of intimate family secrets in specific physiological detail, Mary at last capitulates to Gabriel's wooing. No longer reticent or ironic, not even maidenly demure, Mary surrenders, declaring herself "the slave of the Lord. Let him do with me what he wants."

Gabriel departs and the scene ends so abruptly that the omitted details of this human-divine conception have intrigued us for twenty centuries.

The next we see of Mary, she is hurrying south from Nazareth to visit her cousin in the suburbs of Jerusalem, a trip of several days' duration. As soon as Elizabeth sets eyes on the girl, she recognizes that Mary, still unmarried, is pregnant. Yet Elizabeth honors, rather than reviles, her young cousin. Not in suppressed whispers either, but in a loud voice, calling Mary the mother of her Lord. The child Elizabeth is carrying begins his career as herald in the womb, "leaping" as he recognizes his cousin Jesus.

Mary does not keep quiet in this scene either. Elizabeth's public confirmation both of her pregnancy and her innocence spurs Mary to break forth in song, stitching scraps of psalms together with words remembered from the Old Testament thanksgiving of Hannah, mother of the prophet Samuel. Like Hannah's, Mary's song is highly political, stressing the way God will vindicate and elevate the lowly and powerless, while subjugating the high and mighty. Neither Mary nor her listeners would have made distinctions between spiritual and political realms, however. She is, in fact, echoing Gabriel's message that her son will be the king who restores Israel, affirming publicly what she has been told privately.

Mary stays three months with Elizabeth until her cousin's child is born. Then she returns to Nazareth, just as her own condition is beginning to show. She must have known that her marriage plans would now be in peril.

Understandably, Joseph has a hard time accepting Mary's story. She's just come back from the big city, and she expects him to believe some tale about a mysterious stranger and his shady promises? He can hardly be expected to go through with the marriage now. In fact, he is on the point of settling with her family, putting the best face he can on the matter, when Mary's stranger shows up in Joseph's own dreams, confirming her story and instructing him to continue with the wedding plans.

Before the baby is born, however, they are forced to leave Mary's hometown of Nazareth. The Romans have directed that a census be taken of the population in the area. Heads of households are required to register at the husband's birth-place—which for Joseph meant Bethlehem. Popular imagination pictures them as travelers, with Mary, heavy with child, on the back of a donkey.

Because Joseph was returning to his hometown, they likely stayed with his family till Mary's embarrassing pregnancy came to term. In those days, the word we translate as "inn" also meant "guest room" or "dining room." Since many Palestinian families lived in lean-tos built at the entrance to limestone caves that pock the hills around Bethlehem, Mary's in-laws, embarrassed by her untimely pregnancy, may well have stuck the visiting couple back in the cave where the animals were kept, their only "guest room." Then again, perhaps her in-laws were not unkind, only poor and cramped for space. At any rate, it is in this dark barn-cave, far from home, that the teenage girl labors to give birth among strangers.

The Christmas cards always clean the scene up, concealing any sign of her struggle, the bloody rags, and discarded placenta. Instead of picturing her with swollen lips and sweat-matted hair, they show Mary serene and sanitary. Yet the cave floor would have been littered with manure and urine-soaked straw, and the feed-trough where she laid her baby filled with moldy hay. No doubt the shepherds who found them that night used similar barn-caves themselves, though perhaps not as a nursery.

How did Mary feel as these strange men stood around her gawking? What did she make of their tales about angels singing? And when the sheepherders left, waking the little town with their rowdy excitement, would she have felt vindicated among the strangers who had previously smirked at her own story? She certainly never forgot that night, storing each detail to savor and reflect upon during the days and years that followed.

The new mother has other visitors in Bethlehem. Scholars from the East arrive, bearing gifts for the new baby—gold, some incense, and myrrh: an ointment used to prepare bodies for burial. Strange gifts for an infant. Not very practical. But then what do men—especially academic types—know about babies anyway?

Within eight days, the little family goes to the temple in Jerusalem for the baby's circumcision ceremony. There Mary hears her son's destiny once more publicly confirmed, by an old man, Simeon, and a devout widow, Anna. Both bless her baby and prophesy his future greatness. However, Simeon then turns to Mary and addresses her directly. Though her child will save his people, Simeon predicts this feat will not be without cost. Many will oppose him. And the strife he provokes will bring about the greatest sorrow of his mother's life. Ominous words. They cast a shadow into the future.

The months go by in Bethlehem. Then, suddenly, Mary finds herself uprooted once more. The visiting scholars, it appears, have unwittingly upset the king with their loose talk about her child. In a fit of paranoid rage, the ruler plans to wipe out the infant population around Bethlehem. The angel warns Joseph that they must escape to Egypt. This time there will be no one to take them in, no way to make a living as immigrants in that foreign country. Now Mary sees the sense in that gift of gold the wise men brought.

After a while, the old king dies, and they are free to return to their native country. This time the angel directs them back to Mary's old hometown of Nazareth. After such a long absence, after such adventures, Mary must have greeted her friends and family again with relief. Such strange things have happened to her since that day the stranger appeared so suddenly before her. Now her family is safe in Nazareth again; maybe they can settle down, establish a routine, take up where they'd left off.

These are the "hidden years" in the life of the family. We don't know much about what went on during this period, though we can infer that Mary's house began to fill with children. At least seven, finally, in all. Besides Jesus, there was

James, Joses, Simon, Judas—all named in Matthew's gospel—
and at least two sisters.

Their yearly routine included regular visits south to the
Jerusalem temple at Passover, evidence that Joseph was finan-
cially secure in Nazareth, possibly even prosperous. Entire
villages often made a party of these pilgrimages, traveling
as a group, both for the fun and for safety. Mary always remembered the Jerusalem trip when Jesus was twelve, the year before
his bar mitzvah. On the way back to Nazareth after the celebration, she and Joseph suddenly discover their oldest son
is missing. No one in their large party has seen him since they
left the city. The distraught parents are forced to turn back
and search for him.

When they find the boy, still in the temple, he is surrounded by the temple intellectuals, discussing the Torah with
them as if he had been a little professor himself. Mary's scold-
ing catches the tone of aggrieved motherhood, recognizable
even after twenty centuries: "How could you do this to us?"
she demands of her adolescent son. "Your father and I have
been looking for you everywhere. We were scared to death!"

Her son's response must have shocked them. He says something like "What's the big deal? Didn't you know this is where
I'd be—taking care of my Father's business?"

Whether or not they found his reply impudent, they certainly found it puzzling, Luke tells us. Had all those unevent-
ful years back in Nazareth dimmed the memory of this son's
peculiar birth? Did the angelic messenger seem only a dream
to them now? Jesus goes back to Nazareth and behaves himself after this adolescent rebellion. But Mary must have felt at
least a prick of the sword Simeon had prophesied for her,
enough to make her wonder once more just what might be
in store for this boy of hers.

Twenty more years go by during which we see nothing
else of Mary. All her children were probably grown and some
of them married by the time she appears again. She is quite
possibly a widow now, since Joseph does not appear again,

though the hometown crowd refers to Jesus scornfully as "the carpenter's son"[2] when he tries to preach to them.

Mary, however, is convinced that her eldest son possesses miraculous powers. When they attend a wedding in the next town, Cana, he performs his first miracle at her express request—turning water into wine when the host runs out. At first he resists. In fact, his response to her is testy to the point of rudeness. "Woman," he says, "what have I to do with you?"[3] Then he adds, "It's not my time yet. Don't push it." But with the unflappable maternal faith of a stage mother, Mary ignores him and instructs the servants to do whatever he tells them. She obviously has no idea how he might bring this off, or even if he wants to. But she has serene confidence in his power to do it. And at this point even Jesus seems unable to oppose her wishes.

His hometown, unfortunately, does not share her confidence. So Mary's son leaves home for good and wanders the countryside with his followers, most of them ragtag fishermen from Capernaum. Now Mary, so willing in her youth, so confident at the Cana wedding, begins to have doubts about this touring miracle business. Realizing that her boy can't attract large crowds without also attracting the notice of the officials, she wonders if her son has lost his mind. Already experts from the temple in Jerusalem are checking him out. And the Romans, she knows, have no qualms about punishing people they see as a threat to the security and peace of the empire. Fearing both for his safety and his sanity, Mary goes after him to bring him home again. Here we have another clue that she is a widow now, since it is her other sons rather than her husband who accompany her on this mission.

Think of the family dynamics at work here as well. With Joseph dead, the oldest son is obliged to take over his responsibilities as head of the family. Working in the carpentry shop is obviously not what Jesus has mapped out for his life's work, however. The brothers next in line, James and Joses, are understandably exasperated with their older sibling. Who does he think he is anyway, running off and leaving them to take care of everything—including their mother? He needs to come back home and take over the family business, they would have complained to their mother, not go running around the countryside, making wild claims and upsetting the authorities. Very possibly there are also younger children, sisters whose wedding dowries depend on their older brother taking a hand in things. Now he's deserted them, leaving James and Joses holding the bag. Well, it isn't fair and he's not going to get away with it—not if they have anything to say about it.

Mary would have seen their point. What mother wouldn't— pulled by the competing needs of her other children? Thus we see her, in this early stage of Jesus' itinerant ministry, entreating her wayward son to come back home, to give up these crazy ambitions, to stop his dangerous talk about kingdoms and rulers. After all, look what's happened to his cousin John already. He's in jail and likely to have his head chopped off any day now for inciting riots.

Jesus, for his part, feels his family has let him down. Though they may only mean to establish an insanity defense in case of his arrest, their claims that he is not in his right mind give the Pharisees and other temple functionaries a weapon to use against him. These Jewish leaders begin to plant doubt in the minds of his followers, saying Jesus is possessed by demons.

Thus when his mother and brothers appear outside the house where Jesus is staying and demand to talk to him, he is well aware of their mission. Having experienced his mother's determined tenacity at Cana, he knows what extreme measures it will take to deter her. He answers his family's request, as he so often answered everyone, with a question: "Who are my mother and my brothers?"[4] Then, as he gestures around the room at his followers, he adds, "These are my mother and brothers."

Mary, no doubt, was dumbfounded. How can he do this to her? This isn't mere adolescent rebellion; this is outright rejection. He might as well say, "Depart from me; I never knew you."

Simeon's words come back to haunt Mary as she feels for the first time the sword enter her heart. She returns to Nazareth, heartbroken.

Reports of her son filter back to Mary there in the backwater town. No doubt she finds it ironic that he consistently extols the fifth commandment, *Honor thy father and mother*, calling the Pharisees hypocrites for ignoring the spirit of the Law by pledging to their favorite charity while refusing to support their aged parents. He tells rich, young executives to take care of their mother and father, but is he following his own advice? Your first duty, he's telling his followers, is to your heavenly Father. Yet she remembers how, even as a child, he claimed to be tending to that Father's business.

When she hears the next part of this teaching, however, she feels the sword twist: "If any man come to me, and hate not his father, and mother, and wife, and children, and brethren, and sisters, yea, and his own life also, he cannot be my disciple."[5] Strong words. The hardest of all for a mother.

Then, on Jesus' last visit home, he and his brothers tangle over whether he should go to Jerusalem for the harvest festival that fall. The Feast of Booths was the biggest celebration of the year. Rabble-rousers of every stripe came to Jerusalem then, certain of finding a large, excitable audience. "Exactly your kind of place," his brothers tell him. "Why hide here in Galilee, making life hard for us, when you could be in the big city, raising Cain? If you want to make a name for yourself, that's the place to be."

Mary knows they are merely baiting him, of course. They never have believed in him. To her other sons, he is just the big brother, always lording it over them. And she is always in the middle, trying to keep peace in the family.

For her part, Mary has never doubted her son's power. She proved that at the wedding in Cana. Surely he knows she's on his side. What she doesn't understand is the purpose of that power. He's not using it to make them rich. He doesn't even seem interested in freeing his people either from the Romans or those bureaucrats in Jerusalem who make their lives so hard here in the provinces. Why not? Wasn't she led to believe that's what would happen by the stranger and the sheepherders and the Eastern academics? It's still a puzzle to her, ponder it as she will.

She has not forgotten how oddly this son came into the world or how his life was mysteriously preserved. Yet long stretches of ordinary life affect our memory of the extraordinary; that sense of heightened reality the angel brought was hard to recreate now. With Joseph no longer around to corroborate those memories, they have slipped away into some dreamlike realm. The others who had been there, who had borne witness to those singular events—the sheepherders, the Eastern scholars—where are they now? Anna and Simeon, those prophets of her son's greatness, both are dead. All she has now are her squabbling children and these fragile memories.

Despite the outrage of her other children, Mary fears for the safety of her eldest child. She doesn't fully understand what he is up to. But then who does? Even those boys of Zebedee who seem to have taken the place of his own flesh and blood, they seem as puzzled as anyone. Their mother told her only recently how she'd tried to nail Jesus down, get him to promise her boys a prime appointment when he turned the rascals in Jerusalem out and took over himself. Jesus had only told her she didn't know what she was asking for.

Then something changes. Maybe Mrs. Zebedee's leaving home to find Jesus on behalf of her own sons gave Mary an idea. Maybe she heard he was surrounding himself with women who were no better than they ought to be and thought she could at least protect him from their wiles. Maybe she got tired of James and Joses bossing her around and constantly criticizing her beloved boy. Maybe she just missed him. We don't know when or how Mary left home. We only know that

at one point she decides to join her eldest son on his pil-
grimage to Jerusalem because she is named in all four gospels
as being among the women who followed Jesus from Galilee
to the cross.

The three synoptic gospels—Mark, Matthew, and Luke—
identify her at this point as "Mary the mother of James and
Joses" or "Mary the mother of James the less and Joses." Since
people had no last names as we know them, they were routinely identified by formulas of relationship—"the son of,"
"the wife of," etc. Mary's not being identified as "wife of Joseph"
is one of the reasons we assume she is now a widow. But why
is she no longer identified as she was earlier as "the mother
of Jesus"? John's gospel supplies the reason for this switch.

Mary is a widow, dependent now on her other children.
She has very possibly risked their displeasure to leave home
and follow this son, the troublemaker. Resentful of their older
sibling, they are indignant at Mary's willful defiance of propriety and good sense. Let her go traipsing around the countryside if she likes, but don't expect them to welcome her back
with open arms when this whole fiasco comes to its disastrous
end. *Be it unto me according to thy will,*[6] she'd said to the stranger
that day, never dreaming she would lose the very son she'd
been given, nor that the ones who came later would reject her.

As Jesus hung on the cross, one of his final acts is to discharge his filial responsibility. He realizes that as eldest son
his duty is indeed to provide for his mother. What will happen to her now that the son she's left home for—not once but
twice now—is determined to die, leaving her alone and unpro-
tected? His angry brothers may not take her in again. Jesus,
therefore, in a mutual-adoption ceremony, bestows the responsibility for his mother's care on John, his best-loved disciple.

"Woman," he calls her again, just as he had at Cana where
she had made her untimely claims on him, "behold thy son."[7]

Woman. Ishah. The name of Eve as well as Mary. He was
speaking not only to his own mother but to all mothers since
the first one. All the children you thought you'd lost—from

Abel and Cain to Jesus—they are restored to you. The children on whom you've lavished your love, expended your nights and days, for whom you've given up your own life—here they are. Just as he had called his disciples his kin on that terrible day when he seemed to reject her, he now calls those same disciples her children, the ones she can count on to care for her. *From that hour that disciple took her unto his own home.*[8]

At the very moment Mary needed it most, when the sword was plunged up to its hilt in her heart, watching her son die, she was at last included in that circle of followers he had drawn around himself, a circle she thought had excluded her. But once she followed him, it opened to her also.

Therefore, this is not the last we see of Mary. She helps take down her son's battered body from the cross; she is also a witness to his resurrection. She returns to the upper room with the disciples after Jesus' ascension. And she is called once more "Mary the mother of Jesus."

Not only is this son restored to her, however. She has become an evangelist. Because with her among the disciples are her other sons. And how else should these unbelievers, these scoffers, these siblings who would not be reconciled to their brother in life be reunited with him now, except through the good offices of their mother? In fact, it is James, her second son, who becomes the head of the church in Jerusalem, mediating between the Gentile Christians and the conservative Jerusalem Jews. This son Mary would also lose, according to the historian Josephus, martyred for love of his brother and Lord.

But perhaps by then, gaining and losing had all become one to Mary, a part of the bigger picture. The one all mothers struggle to focus on, where joy of conception turns to pain of childbirth, then becomes almost idolatrous joy as their children grow and wax strong in favor with God and man, the pain returning as those children leave home, a loss that can only be fully redeemed within the circle of those who follow Mary's son.

Women and Marriage

Unlike motherhood, marriage has changed enormously since ancient times. Even between the age of the patriarchs and that of the kings, marriage customs changed, then altered even more drastically when the Middle East fell under the control of Rome.

From the earliest times, Hebrews considered marriage the normative state for all adults. The Old Testament, in fact, contains no word for "bachelor." Existence being a good deal more precarious then, the community's need to propagate overrode individual preference. It was a father's particular obligation to find a husband for his daughter. Marriage was perceived more often than not as a business deal, though romance and tenderness are not lacking from certain marriage tales of this period. The story of Rachel and Jacob is probably the most famous of these.

But polygamy was also a part of this collective procreative urge. Not only were female slaves sexually available to the master of the household, but he could take on as many wives as he could support. In addition, concubines occupied a rather nebulous position somewhere between wife and slave. These quasi wives could also bear children with legal claims on their father's estate. A number of the Bible's tales of marriage are based on the inevitable jealousies such a tangle of relationships produced, often compounded by a first wife's infertility.

Polygamy had died out in Palestine by the time of the New Testament. Divorce, however, still made multiple marriages possible; they simply had to be sequential rather than simultaneous. And Roman law allowed what Jewish law had not—the right of a woman to divorce her husband. The Samaritan woman Jesus meets at Jacob's well illustrates how little this prerogative benefited her.

Most of the women mentioned in the gospels are either widows or single. Some women even appear to have taken Jesus seriously and left their homes and families to follow him. Many of the women the Apostle Paul relied on so heavily during his ministry were also widows. Thus we have surprisingly few glimpses of New Testament marriages.

This is not to say that marriage is not held in high regard in Christian scriptures, however. Jesus not only attended weddings but taught about marriage in ways that recognized the full moral agency of women. Yet his response to women is never based on their marital status, but on their individual need. Perhaps the picture of marriage most attractive to contemporary women is that of Prisca and Aquila, who survived exile, worked as business partners, and traveled widely together to spread the gospel.

RUTH
Ruth 1–4

*E*xcept for Esther, Ruth is the only book in the Bible named for a woman. It's unusual in other ways also. The story contains more dialogue than any other biblical book, giving it the dramatic quality of a play. Yet no villain appears in any of the four scenes; the plot complication arises only from harsh circumstance. Nor does God speak or act directly in this story. None of Ruth's characters are warriors, priests, prophets, or kings. It is entirely a domestic tale of two women—Naomi and her daughter-in-law Ruth, the reversals they suffer, and how they manage to salvage their fortunes by their own wits.

The story takes place sometime after Moses led the descendants of Abraham out of slavery in Egypt to the Promised Land, where the tribes live in a loose confederation, ruled not by kings but by judges who arbitrate disputes and, if need be, lead them in battle. Almost totally an agricultural society, the people depend on the land and the weather. In fact, one of the periodic famines that beset the region sets our tale in motion.

Naomi and her husband Elimelech of Bethlehem take their two sons and flee the famine by immigrating to Moab on the eastern side of the Dead Sea where the people worship the god Chemosh, sometimes with human sacrifices. The move, unfortunately, does not improve Elimelech's health; he dies there in Moab, far from home. The two sons, with the not very promising names Mahlon ("Weakness") and Kilion ("Perishing"), marry Moabite women, Orpah and Ruth. The two wives and their mother-in-law get along exceptionally well and form strong bonds to one another. When, despite the attentive nursing of their mother and wives, the sons die, the bonds of affection between the women survive.

Naomi now finds herself alone in a strange land without the support of male kin and no way to make a living. Hearing that the famine at home in Judah has broken, she sets out for Bethlehem. Though under no particular obligation to do so, her two daughters-in-law accompany her. Knowing the dangers of travel, Naomi is probably grateful for their companionship, yet she also knows they will not be welcomed in her own homeland. Thus, probably when they reach the border, she thanks them for their kindness and asks God's blessing on them, but tells them to go back to their own mothers' homes. They're still young. They can find new husbands.

In tears, both women protest that they will leave their own people for her. Embittered by her own losses and frustrated by her impotence, Naomi is forced to spell things out for them. "Think about it," she says, "at my age, what man's going to give me a second look? And even supposing by some miracle I got married today and pregnant tonight, are you going to wait around for two of my babies to grow up so you can marry them? Not very likely! Go home. You've still got your looks—which is more than I have. You've still got a chance. I've got nothing. Everything the good Lord gave me he's taken away."

We should not be surprised that Naomi talks like this; she's only speaking from her heart, echoing dark sentiments often recorded in the Psalms. These ancient people were never bashful nor dishonest about how they felt about God. Naomi has seen her entire family wiped out. She has very little to look forward to, even when she returns to her homeland. The one thing she can still do is save these two young women who are like daughters to her from her own sorry fate. Consequently, she puts the case to them in the strongest terms she can muster.

With Orpah it works. Still weeping, she turns back to Moab. Ruth, however, is more tenacious. She refuses to leave Naomi alone. In one of those ironies of literary history, Ruth's poetic speech has found its way into countless wedding ceremonies as an expression of unquenchable love: "Entreat me not to leave thee . . . whither thou goest I will go."[1] But these were words addressed, not to a man, but to another woman, and to a mother-in-law at that.

Finally Naomi relents, and she and Ruth enter Bethlehem together in springtime, just as the barley harvest is beginning. Naomi's return after ten years causes quite a stir. "How you've changed," everyone tells her.

"You have no idea," she replies, and recounts her tale of woe, insisting that her old friends no longer call her Naomi ("Pleasant") but Mara, a name that means "bitterness."

Meanwhile, Ruth is looking about her, observing how things are done here in Judah. Since the harvest has begun, she figures they won't starve if she can at least go out to the fields and pick up the stalks of grain left behind or dropped by the harvesters, a practice called gleaning. Such leftovers were specifically reserved for the poor and widows, allowing them a little more dignity than rummaging in garbage dumpsters does poor people today.

Nevertheless, harvest crews are a rough bunch, and young women with no protectors were often assaulted in the fields. Therefore, when Boaz, the landowner, turns up to oversee his men, Ruth feels safer, especially when she sees him talking to the harvest foreman and pointing in her direction. Naomi has already told her that Boaz is related to her dead husband. Ruth realizes she must have caught the landowner's eye.

The foreman reports to Boaz that Ruth has worked hard all morning, only stopping once to rest in the shade. Impressed, Boaz approaches Ruth himself. He's an older man, around Elimelech's age, and his advice to her sounds avuncular. "Stay in my field," he tells her, "and stick close to my servant girls. My men won't bother you, not if they know what's good for them. When you get thirsty, go ask one of them and he'll let you drink from our water jugs."

Ruth thanks him lavishly, noting that his generosity extends to her, a foreigner. Not to be outdone, Boaz replies that he's heard of her generosity as well, how she has left everything to help Naomi. He also blesses her, calling on the Lord to cover her with his wings.

Later in the day, Boaz invites Ruth into the shade where the harvest crew is eating. Such an invitation in itself signals his particular interest in the young widow, but he goes further and personally serves her plate, an exceptional act for any man, especially an older, wealthy one. As the crew goes back to work after the meal, he instructs his men to pull stalks of grain from their sheaves and let them fall where Ruth can easily find them. At the end of the day, he sends her home with a tubful of grain, enough to feed her and Naomi for at least a week.

When her mother-in-law hears whose field Ruth has been working in and that Boaz wants her to continue there throughout the harvest, she's ecstatic. Neither woman could have been blind to the signs of special favor Boaz has shown Ruth that day. At this point in the story, Ruth seems happy merely to have their day-to-day survival insured by the patronage of this rich kinsman. The wheels in her mother-in-law's head, however, have already begun to turn. Boaz is, in fact, close enough kin to be designated a *go'el* or "redeemer," either of his dead relation's property or name, according to the levirate law. A *go'el* can even be required to marry his kinsman's childless widow in order to carry on the family line. Naomi, however, does not reveal her plan to Ruth at this point. She only reiterates that gleaning is indeed dangerous work for a woman and that Ruth should stick close to Boaz's servant girls for protection. But she has a further reason for encouraging her daughter-in-law's chaste circumspection.

Ruth continues to work through the months of harvest, the very picture of industry and prudence. While she is aware that Boaz is watching her, she makes no further demands on him. She is, after all, despite having married into his family, clearly a foreigner, and to presume too much would be unseemly.

Meanwhile, Naomi decides to put on the market a field owned by Elimelech, her dead husband. With no money to hire help, she is in no position to work the land herself, of course. She is assured of a sale, since, by law, her deceased husband's next-of-kin *go'el* is obliged to buy the parcel. On the face of it, this may look like a fairly straightforward business deal. But Naomi has something much greater than a field in mind. She is plotting a marriage between her daughter-in-law and Boaz.

After three months of watching the two during the harvest, Naomi doubts that either of them would object. However, Boaz seems a little backward and needs a nudge in the right direction. Therefore, one evening when Ruth returns from the fields, Naomi instructs her daughter-in-law to bathe, put on her best clothes, dab on some perfume, and stroll on down to the threshing floor where the barley is being winnowed.

This part of the harvest, after the grain was in and the landowner assured of a good crop as the mounds of winnowed grain grew higher, tended to be a time of rather generous rejoicing, accompanied by copious refreshments. Ruth is to linger in the shadows until Boaz has eaten and drunk enough to get sleepy. Then, when he's asleep, she is to go to him, uncover his feet, and lie down with him—a rather bold maneuver.

Nevertheless, Ruth follows her mother-in-law's instructions. Boaz, content with his harvest and somewhat elevated by the circulating wineskin, finally curls up and goes to sleep. When he wakes in the middle of the night, he is shocked to find the Moabite woman, who has established a reputation for prudence, lying at his feet on the threshing floor.

This is a rather forthright declaration of her intention, one she immediately makes even plainer: "Cover me," she says to him. "You have the right. Even the obligation."

And Boaz shows himself equal to the delicacy of the moment. Ruth is in fact risking her good reputation with him, a reputation she has spent all summer establishing. Boaz acknowledges this: "You could have had any of the young men you wanted, from the harvest hands on up to the landowners. They've all seen you. They know you're not just some foreign floozy, ready to tumble in the hay. And now that you come to me like this, instead of one of them, well, I take that as a kindness."

There is, however, a hitch, he tells her. Another man, unnamed, actually has a closer degree of kinship, a second cousin instead of a third perhaps. "But lie down," he whispers, "I'll think of something."

The next morning, before daylight, she gets up to leave before they are discovered together. But before she goes, he wants to make her a present. Scooping up six measures of grain from the winnowed mound—all she could carry—he fills her long veil and she slips back within the town gates to Naomi.

Now all the two women can do is wait. Naomi is sure of her man, however. He's used to getting what he wants, she tells Ruth.

Boaz may have been bashful before, but emboldened now, he goes to the city gate, comparable to our city hall, and confronts the unnamed kinsman along with a quorum of city councilmen. Naomi, he craftily points out, wants to sell the portion of land she's inherited from her husband. Is the kinsman prepared to buy it?

The fellow thinks it over and decides yes, he will.

Fine, says Boaz. But that means you also have to marry Ruth, the Moabite daughter-in-law, as well and get her pregnant so that Elimelech's line won't die out. What he doesn't say, but what the kinsman quickly figures out, is that the very field he's just offered to buy would then go not to his own children but to the child Ruth would bear. He'd actually be losing on the deal then, paying for land he would never own.

His response then is exactly what Boaz had hoped for. "Changed my mind," he says. "Right now I just can't see my way clear to buy that field of Naomi's. If you want it, go ahead. It's yours."

"You're sure about that?" Boaz persists.

So eager is the other man to escape what is obviously an unprofitable business proposition, that, to seal the deal, he pulls off his sandal before the ten city councilmen, a sign of his relinquishment of the "rights" of the redeemer.

"Fine," says Boaz. "Then I'll do it." And he calls all the crowd who've gathered, as well as the councilmen, to witness his willingness to buy the field, to marry Ruth, to carry out the responsibilities to Elimelech's family. What the other man, obviously of a stingier nature, saw as a diminishment, Boaz sees as an enlargement. The people meet his magnanimous gesture with praise, comparing him to their patriarch Judah.

When in due time Ruth bears her first son, he is called Obed and given to her mother-in-law as a replacement for those sons she lost in Moab. Naomi's own happiness is thus restored by the gratifying union she's engineered between Ruth and Boaz. But the story doesn't end here, because a genealogical tag ties it to the future. Obed, we're told, child of Ruth and Boaz, child also of Naomi and Elimelech, child of Rachel and Leah, Tamar and Judah, child of Israel, child of promise, becomes grandfather of David, king of Israel.

What a strange picture of marriage all this is for us to take in. Most modern treatments of this book turn Ruth into a Gothic romance, following the pattern we find in novels from

Jane Eyre to Barbara Cartland, in which a vulnerable heroine with few resources is rescued by a mysterious, rich champion. We like our damsels to be distressed and our heroes to be their rescuers. This is the part we understand best about the story.

What we don't understand very well, what seems almost barbaric to us, is the practice of levirate marriage, the custom that provides the hinge for the story. The anonymous relative with the nearer degree of kinship supplies the last dramatic obstacle to the fulfillment of this romance. The way Boaz contrives to take the other man's place shows us how much he desires Ruth. But though we may be pleased with the outcome, the notion of marrying a brother-in-law or a cousin by marriage just to conceive so the family name can continue takes the bloom off the romance for us. We want to be treasured for ourselves alone. The physical fruits of marriage, though desired by most women, are for us a separate issue altogether. Newly married women today feel irritated, even personally demeaned, when friends or relatives ask if they're pregnant yet. At least intellectually we separate our worth as women, as persons, from our fecundity.

To the Israelites, however, having the family line cut off was tantamount to cosmic extinction. Producing offspring assured a tangible afterlife, not just for yourself but for your entire family. Children were not a personal choice. They were the extension of one's whole clan into the future. Thus Tamar,[2] to whom Ruth is compared in this story, after her husband died leaving her childless, took the terrible risk of disguising herself as a prostitute and enticing her father-in-law Judah to impregnate her. Like Naomi, Tamar was forced to be shrewd, demanding a pledge from Judah until he paid his bill, personal items that she could then use to defend herself against the death penalty for fornication when her pregnancy began to be obvious.

Barrenness was the worst fate that could befall a woman. *Intentional* childlessness was unthinkable. Women would pursue almost any avenue rather than remain in such a state, Tamar's story being an extreme example. But women like Hannah who wept and prayed for a child at the Shiloh shrine must have been fairly common. To have a child, especially a son, was not simply a private joy but a participation in vast destiny. That's why Ruth's marriage to Boaz is so important to Naomi. Not only will the two women be able to live in comfort now, but the loss Naomi experienced in the deaths of her husband and sons is stanched. The first child from this union will, in a kind of metaphysical gene-splicing, be her own extension into the future of the cosmos, a prospect that includes a king.

But there is an important difference between the story of Ruth and that of Tamar. Tamar's is a tale of brutal degradation. Even the participants recognize that to preserve the family line, the individual woman has paid a terrible cost. Ruth's story, on the other hand, shows the desires of the individual and the good of the community happily coinciding. Ruth's womb is indeed a conduit through which history will flow, and she is fulfilling her obligation to her dead husband's family by submitting to levirate marriage. However, the middle scenes with their delicate courtship maneuvers common to men and women in love also show that marrying just any old cousin wasn't enough. The destiny of these two individual people, Ruth and Boaz, matters as much as the continuation of the bloodline. Likewise, the care of the two women for one another also makes individual destinies as important as the future prospects of the group.

How is the story brought to its happy conclusion? By wiliness—a characteristic valued by these ancient peoples at least as much as strength or beauty was valued by the Greeks. Ruth undertakes to make a living for herself and Naomi, showing admirable grit. Then, recognizing the difficult situation she's in as an outsider, she bides her time, prudently building a reputation that puts her above reproach in the community. Naomi acts as her confidante and guide, providing her with the final, risky plan to declare herself to Boaz. And Boaz himself has to orchestrate the public conclusion to the romance.

The Bible offers no censure of this sort of strategizing. Ruth, Naomi, and Boaz are, after all, only following in the footsteps of the crafty Abraham, the scheming Rebekah, the wily Jacob. Here, in fact, is one instance where all things, including human craft and cultural mores, do indeed work together for good to those who are called according to the grand design of the universe, domestic happiness in harmony with cosmic destiny.

MICHAL AND ABIGAIL

Abigail—1 Samuel 25

Michal—1 Samuel 18:17–19:24, 25:43-44; 2 Samuel 3:1-21, 6

his is a story that begins like a fairy tale. The countryside is being ravaged by marauding Philistines, among whom is the giant Goliath. The king calls for a champion to fight the giant, offering the hand of his daughter as a prize to whoever defeats him. David, though the youngest of eight brothers and still a stripling, responds to the challenge and kills the giant using only a sling-shot and pebbles.

The next episode continues the fairy-tale pattern. The people, overjoyed by their deliverance from the Philistines, praise this unlikely hero as he returns from battle. The women dance in the streets, inventing songs that make unpleasant comparisons between the boy David and Saul the king. Understandably jealous, the king reneges on his promise to give his oldest daughter, Merab, to David, marrying her instead to another man. David, however, does not angrily protest that she by rights belongs to him. Merab may have been too old for him anyway or simply not his type. At any rate, he humbly declares that he's just a poor sheepherder, not really fit to marry into a royal family.

Michal, however, Saul's younger daughter who is closer to David's age, falls in love with the handsome peasant boy when her father sets him up as the court musician. When word of their romance comes to the king, he devises a way to use the young couple's attraction to his advantage. Secretly, he instructs his servants to encourage the relationship, even to suggest to David that he offer to marry Michal.

But like the younger brother in fairy tales, David is nobody's fool. For one thing, a marriage proposal included proffering a "bride-price" to the woman's family, something like a reverse dowry. David protests that he is too poor to afford the large bride-price a princess would require. But Saul is clever too. The king springs his trap: If David will bring him foreskins cut from a hundred Philistines, he will accept them as the bride-price for his daughter Michal. Of course, like any fairy-tale king, Saul believes the young hero has no hope of surviving such an assignment and only sets him the task in order to rid himself of the pesky upstart.

David, however, returns from this commission with double the number of required foreskins—from two hundred Philistine men. The king, of course, can no longer deny him without losing face. David marries Michal, who is more smitten than ever with her young lover.

David continues to lead successful raiding parties against the Philistines; the crowds love him. Even Jonathan, Saul's eldest son and heir to the throne, falls under his influence. The king grows ever more distraught by the shift in everyone's affections. Not only do his people prefer David, but his own family members are enthralled by him. Even God, it seems, has abandoned Saul for David.

After several unsuccessful attempts are made on his life in his father-in-law's court, David slips away in the night and returns to his own house where Michal is waiting for him. She tells him he won't be safe even there, though; he must flee the country altogether. Knowing that her father's spies are already watching the house, she lets her husband down on a rope from her window so that he can escape. Then she stuffs the clay body of an idol under the blanket on the bed and arranges goat hair on the pillow to look like David's. When the king's messengers demand to see her husband, she claims he is sick, giving them a peek at the decoy in the bed.

When the guards report to the king, Saul smells a rat. "I don't care how sick he is. Bring him to me, even if you have to carry him here in the bed."

When the guards return for David, Michal's subterfuge is discovered. Saul is furious. "How could you do this to me?" he shouts at her. "You're siding with my enemy."

"David told me he'd kill me if I didn't help him escape," she tells her father.

Meanwhile, her husband has fled to the only person he feels can help him now—Samuel, the old prophet at Ramah who anointed him. Saul sends his henchmen to capture David there. But as soon as they see Samuel, they find themselves entirely out of control—whirling in circles, spouting words they don't understand, falling down and foaming at the mouth. Saul sends three sets of assassins to Ramah, but all meet the same fate. Finally, in desperation, the king comes himself—only to meet the same fate. In a fit of involuntary ecstasy, he strips off his clothes and falls to the ground in front of Samuel. All day and night he lies there naked, exposed for all the world to see, publicly humiliated.

The king returns home, inflamed by implacable hatred for his son-in-law. David is now a hunted man. He knows that the king is likely to retaliate against his family back in Bethlehem. Therefore, he sends word for his parents and siblings to join him in his mountain stronghold where he is gathering a force of malcontents—mostly the poor and dispossessed in the land. His only means of supporting himself, his family, and his ragamuffin band is to provide protection for the farmers in the surrounding countryside from roving bands of raiders. In turn, the farmers supply David and his company with survival provisions.

The one person David cannot protect from the wrath of his father-in-law, however, is Michal, his young wife. She is now a virtual hostage of the king. Not only is she cut off from her husband and exposed to Saul's wrath, but her father has also lost his mind. That escapade has made him the laughingstock of the kingdom. People even make jokes about him "prophesying" in the nude.

Meanwhile, Michal's husband seems to be having the time of his life playing Robin Hood up in the mountains. He's no longer just a stripling boy, but a force to be reckoned with. Even the kings of the surrounding territories see this. Some of them hire him and his ragtag soldiers as mercenaries. Others, finding him and his guerrilla band a loose cannon in the region, set traps for him, though so far he's managed to outwit all their conspiracies against him. One thing hasn't changed though. He's still poor, living hand to mouth, depending on the local farmers to provide for him and his men.

In fact, it's just such a rich farmer, Nabal, who provides David with his second wife. Nabal, who pastures several thousand head of sheep and goats in the wilderness that David and his men have been patrolling, has brought his herds in for the spring shearing. Since shearing is a traditional time for hospitality and feasting, David figures this is a propitious moment to remind the wealthy farmer just how much he owes to the protection of David's patrols. He even enlists the help of Nabal's shepherds to testify to this.

Nabal—whose name means "fool"—has a reputation as a mean-spirited ingrate. "Who's this David character," he sneers at David's emissaries. "He's nothing more than a renegade. If he thinks I'm going to support him just because he's run away from his master, he's got another think coming."

When David hears this surly reply, his temper flares. He orders his men to strap on their swords, and they set out to pillage Nabal's homestead.

Fortunately, however, one of the herdsmen tells Nabal's

wife Abigail what has transpired. He has nothing but praise for David's men and the way they protected the flocks. "You know what a cantankerous son of a gun our master is," he tells her. "We're all going to suffer now just because he won't listen to reason."

Abigail herself is not only reasonable, but clever. And beautiful besides. She knows her husband too well to doubt the herdsman's prediction. So she gathers up as many provisions as she can get together quickly—bread, wine, sheep carcasses, parched corn, raisins, and figs—packs them on donkeys, and without telling Nabal, heads out to intercept David.

When she finds him she dismounts quickly, throws herself on the ground before him, and makes one of the longest speeches by a woman recorded in the Bible. "You have every right to be angry," she apologizes. "My husband's name Fool is well deserved. If I had heard of your request, I could have arranged for provisions for you and your men. As it is, please accept this small token of my esteem I've brought and change your plans for pillaging our farm. Surely you don't want that kind of guilt on your hands.

"I know that the Lord has great things in store for you. So far you have a spotless record even though you've been hunted and hounded throughout the kingdom. It's obvious, however, that you're the apple of God's eye since he's preserved you against all odds." Abigail even manages to work in a clever allusion to David's triumph over Goliath. "One of these days the Lord will sling the lives of your enemies out like pebbles from a slingshot," she says. "Then it's you who'll be in control. So you don't want to spoil that magnificent future by shedding blood recklessly now. This kind of petty revenge would only make you look small."

No doubt sensing that David is on the point of capitulating to her argument, she smiles up at him demurely and adds, "Maybe then, when you're finally king, you'll remember me, your humble maidservant." Abigail's strategy works. David accepts the gifts she's brought and sends her home again, telling her she has nothing to fear from him.

Arriving home, Abigail discovers that Nabal has finished shearing and is throwing a party. Under the influence of the festive wine, his spirits are elevated, for once to the point of jollity. Seeing that he's drunk, Abigail decides to wait till he's sobered up to tell him about her mission. The next morning, suffering from a hangover, Nabal listens horrified as Abigail tells him how narrowly they escaped David's marauders. The shock literally paralyzes Nabal and, after lying immobilized for ten days, he dies.

When David hears of Nabal's death, his gratitude to Abigail for averting his hasty revenge swells. No doubt he also remembers her charm and good looks. At any rate, he sends messengers back to the farmstead, this time with a proposal of marriage. As for Abigail, she must have been charmed by the young guerrilla captain herself. She accepts the proposal eagerly, even though it means leaving her comfortable home and going to live with him in caves and rough mountain outposts.

Abigail, then, becomes David's second wife. He marries another woman as well—Ahinoam, from the town of Jezreel in the mountains where he's holed up. Since her name and hometown are all we know of her, the marriage could merely have been his way of cementing relations with the local populace.

Multiple marriages were, of course, not uncommon either among the Israelites or their pagan neighbors. The patriarch Jacob had been forced to marry Leah before he could marry her younger and more beautiful sister Rachel. Concubines, of course, were another matter. They occupied some nebulous territory between quasi wives and prostitutes on retainer.

Mosaic Law had rules meant to protect women most vulnerable to abuse in what strikes us as barbarous circumstances. For instance, daughters could be sold by their fathers (remember the "bride-price") to prospective husbands. However, a woman was free to leave the husband without penalty if he were displeased with his purchase; he had no right to put her up for sale again himself. In another attempt to ameliorate the brutal consequences of war for women, Deuteronomy orders a man who marries a woman taken as a prisoner of war to allow her a month of mourning for her parents before being required to perform conjugal duties. Her husband was not allowed to sell her afterward, even if she proved sexually unsatisfactory: "thou shalt not make merchandise of her, because thou hast humbled her."[1] Sad words, implying as they do a world of anguish unknown in the modern world.

Or is it? Rape has always been a part of war, though its casualties are not as well documented as the battlefield injuries. Most recently in Bosnia, soldiers were ordered to rape Muslim women specifically to shame them within their own communities. Israelite law, recognizing the exigencies of human life, including warfare, attempted to preserve some measure of dignity for its women victims so that, even though aliens, they could be absorbed with honorable status into the community.

Mosaic Law also guaranteed certain rights in multiple marriages. The first wife's rations of food and clothing, for example, as well as her opportunities to get pregnant, could not be curtailed simply because her husband had taken another, very possibly younger, woman into the household.

Today, of course, we also countenance multiple marriages. The difference is that ours are sequential rather than simultaneous. Nor are divorce settlements always as generous as the rules governing displaced wives. Today women may have a good deal more freedom about entering marriage, but they are not always well protected when they are superseded by another woman. Not only can they be abandoned with relative ease, but they have no guaranteed income for the rest of their lives either. In many ways women could be treated as property in the Old Testament era, especially by their fathers. Once wed, however, they had a certain amount of power, which came from the laws that disallowed their casual disposal.

In those days of sparse population, women were valuable by virtue of their very sex. Recognizing therefore that a woman's children were her most valuable asset, the law even protected the rights of the children of multiple wives— and thus the rights of their mothers. What a woman's sons inherited from their father did not depend on how affectionate her husband happened to feel toward her on any given day. All heirs received equal portions, except for the firstborn, and even he was allowed no more than a double portion. Thus there was no chance of being cut out of a will altogether simply because a wife had been supplanted by a younger woman. Circumscribed as the lives of women were, Israelite women were protected by law to a degree unusual in the ancient world.

When Abigail marries David, however, concerns about inheritance would not have been uppermost in her mind. For one thing, she brings no children with her, only five maidservants. For another, at that point in his career, David had no property to leave his heirs anyway, his family's assets having been confiscated by the king.

Meanwhile, back at the castle, what has become of Michal? The fairy tale isn't working out so well for her. In fact, it's coming apart at the seams. With her husband gone, she languishes in the power of her father the king, who soon discovers a way to punish his daughter for her disloyalty. He gives Michal away to another man. Thus he derives the dual pleasure of humbling his daughter while undermining any claims David may have to the throne as Saul's son-in-law.

The story highlights dissimilarities between Michal and Abigail. The latter the text describes as an exceptionally intelligent woman and illustrates her ingenuity by showing how she responds to the threat of David's attack. Michal also displays her wit when she helps David escape from her father. Yet, caught in the web of court intrigue, she ends up playing the part of a pawn, powerless to affect her destiny. Michal the princess becomes Michal the slave.

Abigail, on the other hand, the farmer's wife living in the backwaters of the kingdom where the people cannot count on the king's protection against marauders, takes control of the situation when she and her people are threatened. In the end she is freed from what must have been a burdensome marriage to a disagreeable man. Also, unlike Michal, who by her own father's decree is led away from court a virtual captive, Abigail, gives herself to David, acting autonomously and without the arbitration of a male mediator. Then she follows her new husband into the wilderness, to share whatever fate awaits him there.

Does the text mean to imply that Michal should have acted in a similar fashion? Should she have been brave enough not only to engineer her husband's escape but to flee with him also? Biblical narrative, being remarkably subtle, rarely comments on the motives of its characters. Unlike, say, Aesop's fables, it does not state a bald moral at the end of the tale. Rather it usually allows the outcome of the story to speak for itself. But by juxtaposing the fate of Abigail with that of Michal in back-to-back verses at the end of chapter twenty-five in 1 Samuel, the text is making an obvious comparison between the fate of these first two wives of David.

Nevertheless, the life of a renegade warrior's wife was not an easy one. Abigail and Ahinoam soon had to leave the guerrilla base camp and move with David's band of now well-trained soldiers into Philistine territory to escape Saul. There David negotiated with Achish, the king of Gath, for the fortified town of Ziklag. Achish, eager to make use of David's troops as mercenaries, granted his request, unaware that David planned to use Ziklag to launch raiding parties along the trading route to Egypt. For almost a year and a half his retinue lives there. Then the crisis David has been dreading arrives. The Philistines, under whose protection he and his entourage now live, decide to attack his homeland, and he is obliged to accompany Achish.

Fortunately, however, some of the other Philistine leaders, suspecting where David's true loyalties may lie, have
refused to fight with him. He returns to Ziklag to find the
town in ashes. In his absence, Amalekites have attacked and
carried off all the women and children, including Abigail and
Ahinoam. Leaving part of his force behind to guard the town,
David and the rest of his men overtake the Amalekites and
rescue the captives.

Meanwhile, the Philistines begin their decisive campaign
against Saul and his son Jonathan at Gilboa, farther north.
Thus David avoids engagement in the final battle that ends
the lives of both Saul his king and Jonathan his friend.

With Saul dead and the Amalekites at least temporarily
subdued, David finds himself in control of the southern region
of the kingdom known as Judah. He moves his headquar-
ters to Hebron where he sets up shop as king. Here his household quickly begins to multiply. Both Ahinoam and Abigail
have sons there. He marries four more women who also bear
children during the seven years he spends in Hebron. Though
only the firstborn sons of each wife are named, we presume
his entourage now burgeons with offspring.

Meanwhile, at least nine years have passed since Michal
last saw David. Even though her father has treated her shame-
fully, the death of Saul comes as a blow to her since it strips
her of whatever protection his royal status may give her. Abner,
the dead king's general, has set up Michal's brother, Ish-
Bosheth, as a puppet king over the northern part of the kingdom, though everyone knows the general still pulls the strings.

In fact, Abner has little faith in Ish-Bosheth's regal abilities and sends messengers to David, inquiring what kind of
deal they can make. And from this low point, Michal's star
seems to rise again. The first thing David asks for as a pledge
of Abner's sincerity is the return of his first wife. Her brother
the puppet king is eager to grant this request and sends for
his sister immediately, though as before, Michal has no voice
in the matter.

And what of Phaltiel, the man who has been her husband for the past nine years? Obviously he loves his princess-bride even though she was out of favor with her father. He follows her procession along the road "weeping behind her."[2] But Abner, who cannot afford an unseemly incident in these delicate political negotiations, turns him back and tells him to go home. Phaltiel has no say in the affair either.

Was there a joyous reunion between Michal and David after all these years? Her first husband is now in his thirties, no longer an impulsive youth but a seasoned warrior and crafty politician. Has his affection for her waned as he matured and acquired a kingdom and six more wives, women who have produced plenty of offspring for him? (Michal had borne no children before David's banishment from the kingdom.) Was his request for Michal's restitution merely a political ploy, a means of cementing his monarchical claims by reaffirming his membership in Saul's family?

Again, this is one of those places where the Bible is mute about its characters' motivations. The only testimony we have are those impotent tears of her second husband, Phaltiel, and one unpleasant scene between Michal and David after her restoration.

Both as the dead king's daughter and as the new king's first wife, Michal would rule the domestic roost at the palace. Powerless for so long, used as a sexual pawn in a political game, Michal's sudden release from impotence and her elevation to first lady could not help but affect her. The other wives and their children have to answer to her now. Finally, she's in the driver's seat.

"Too long a sacrifice makes a stone of the heart," the poet Yeats wrote millennia later. And it seems possible that this is what has happened to Michal. She saved her beloved David when he was just a boy, sacrificing her marriage, her happiness, eventually her very body. She has not even had the vindication of children as Phaltiel's wife. Surrounded now by women who know her husband far better than she does, who have proved fruitful while she remains barren, her spirit turns sour, though again, Michal's inner world is presented to us only by the way she enacts it openly.

David, now ensconced in Jerusalem as king over the entire united kingdom, is eager to bring to his city the Ark of the Covenant, the central religious symbol that contains the stone tables of the commandments. To house it, he sets up before the palace a special tent, a replica of the one that had covered it during his ancestors' wanderings in the wilderness. The entrance of the Ark into the city is to be surrounded with music and great pageantry. Dancers like those who had celebrated her father's and her husband's military triumphs are to accompany the Ark. Michal's status and sex, however, preclude her participation in the festivities.

As the street crowds roar outside, Michal the queen sits in the palace at her window, looking on. Suddenly the crowd parts and she sees, not a troupe of dancing women, but her husband the king, whirling like a dervish in a most undignified way. No sense of propriety, of decorum! Perhaps the unpleasant memory of her father, prophesying in insensible ecstasy, surfaces then. She recalls how Saul stripped himself and lay naked for all the world to see on that day when he brought the fortunes of his family crashing down around their ears.

Meanwhile, David is laughing and singing in the streets, dispensing gifts to the crowds like candy. Michal looks down at the spectacle in disgust. She despises the sight of her husband leaping up and down like that. Why, you can see everything! All those women hanging on him—it's disgraceful. Michal sits and fumes, impotent once more.

After the celebration, when everyone has eaten and drunk his fill and gone home, David returns to his palace to celebrate in private with his household. This has been a great day for him, a fulfillment of all those long years hiding out in the mountains, fighting and finagling to keep his ragtag band alive, holding on to hope when there seemed to be none.

Finally he has united not only his people but the Lord with his people, too. But what greets him as he comes through the door brings a sudden end to his high spirits. By now Michal has worked herself into a fury. A nasty marital quarrel ensues that stirs up old hurts and grievances.

"Oh, you looked every inch a king today," she says, venom in her voice. "And the whole world could see every inch too. You looked like some kind of flasher out there. What were you doing—trying to impress the girls with your machismo?"

David is stunned. His heart, so high only moments before, plummets. He looks at this woman, the representative of the forces that hounded him and tried to deny him this triumph, and listens to her mocking him. Then his own fury erupts. "Great," he says, "just great. Well, you may think you're an expert on royal etiquette, sweetheart, but let me tell you something. It was me the Lord chose when that lousy father of yours screwed things up. It was *me* God wanted, not him—nor anybody from his whole lousy family. So if I want to kick up my heels and celebrate, I'm sure not going to let some has-been princess lecture me on manners. And if you were shocked by seeing a little skin today, that ain't nothing to what you're going to see. I'm obviously not good enough for Miss Princess. But I'm sure I can satisfy those little dancing girls."

And with that, the marriage of David and Michal was, for all intents and purposes, at an end. She lived on at the palace, still the queen, but she remained childless, a wife in name only. As the years passed, did she take a grim pleasure in watching the tragedy that befell her erstwhile husband's household? Did the aging Michal rejoice when the lovely Bathsheba's baby, the fruit of her husband's adultery, died?

And that was only the beginning of the catastrophes.

David's other children, born to the women he accumulated in Hebron, weren't able to get along either. They later turned to incest, murder, and finally rebellion against their father the king. Amnon, his firstborn, raped his half-sister Tamar. (See Tamar's story, pages 112–116.) In revenge, Absalom, David's third son, killed Amnon. When he was banished from the court for his crime, he fomented a rebellion against David, forcing the king to flee Jerusalem. Later Absalom himself was killed in a battle with David's forces. Adonijah, David's fourth son, was executed by his half-brother Solomon when he became king for conspiring against Solomon's ascension to the throne. Did Michal feel vindicated then? We don't know. The harem was, after all, a private place, and its secrets remain undisclosed. It was, as we still say today, the children who suffered.

From what we see of David's eight wives, Abigail had probably the best marriage of them all. After Nabal's death, she was able to take that most unusual step for women in the ancient world and choose a husband for herself. She didn't waste this opportunity by opting for wealth or security. Marrying David meant taking on a life of hardship in his mountain stronghold. This required some courage and no little sacrifice.

When her husband's fortunes later improved, no doubt she continued to act with the same wisdom that had once saved the lives of her farmhands and herself. After all, her first marriage to a difficult man had no doubt sharpened her survival skills. Abigail's son was one of the few children in the royal family who did not suffer some tragedy.

Interestingly, the text records no overt sign of jealousy among these wives. Though we tend to shrug off the bitterness of polygamy, chalking our discomfort up to cultural conditioning, David's wives weren't necessarily immune to resentment and rivalry for his affections. Perhaps their children's dark doom was merely the public reflection of their private rancor. The mention of Michal's childlessness may itself indicate her loss of status in the harem.

Nothing is so evanescent in marriage as romantic love. It either deepens into something stronger or disappears altogether. Women who have been divorced know the particular pain of this reality. Being superseded in a husband's affections is hard for any woman to swallow. Nevertheless, women, particularly those with a strong sense of their own competence like Abigail, manage to move forward with their lives. White House wives like Eleanor Roosevelt and Jackie Kennedy no doubt had to learn the lesson of Abigail. Divorced women today handle the trauma of rejection by finishing degrees, going back to work, learning some new skill. It is possible for a woman to step out of the batting lineup of a multiple marriage and play another, more rewarding game.

The children, however, can't. Their relationship with their father is not at an end just because the marriage is. It continues, and, especially if other children by other mothers are in the picture, they feel a constant uneasiness as to how they weigh in the scales of their father's affection compared to their half-siblings. (Of course, the same can be said for siblings with the same parents, but that uncertainty is magnified in multiple marriages.)

Polygamy now seems an archaic custom (though a fair amount of the world's population still practice it). We tend to focus on sexual aspects of these marriages—the jealousies engendered by daily life in the harem. While these probably occurred, they are not what the Bible emphasizes. When we look at the bitter end of this family saga, what we see are brothers and sisters turned against one another and against their father.

SAMARITAN WOMAN

John 4

*B*etween Jesus' hometown of Nazareth in the Galilee district and the city of Jerusalem, about seventy miles to the south as the raven flew, lay a sector called Samaria. Though important to the natives, these geographical distinctions meant little to the Romans who had combined the entire region into one province. All the emperor back in Rome knew—or cared—about the Palestinian region was that complex religious controversy continually racked it, often breaking out into bloody conflict between rival parties.

Shortly after the union between Samaria and Judea, for instance, a gang of Samaritan activists desecrated the temple in Jerusalem during Passover by scattering bones inside the sacred compound. Samaritan partisans struck again in AD 52, massacring a group of Galilean pilgrims making their way through Samaria to Jerusalem. The Roman government had enough headaches dealing with the profusion of religions in the vast territories it had conquered; all it asked of Herod, its puppet king in Palestine, was that he somehow maintain peace in the region.

To the Jews living in the province, however, the geographical divisions of Samaria, and Judea signified a significant break in their spiritual heritage. Though Samaritans were descendants of the original ten northern tribes of Israel, they were not even called Jews at the time of Jesus. Like tourists avoiding the ghettos of cities by staying on elevated interstates, orthodox Jews from the north would go out of their way to skirt Samaria by taking a more westerly route along the coast or crossing over to the east side of the Jordan when traveling south to Jerusalem.

Nevertheless, certain shrines in Samaria, dating back even before Moses to the patriarchs, remained important to the Jews. At Shechem, for instance, both Abraham and Jacob had built altars; the Israelites had carried the bones of Joseph all the way from Egypt and had buried them there. At Shechem, too, Joshua gave his farewell address, and God had renewed the covenant he made with Moses at Sinai. Deborah, the woman who was judge over Israel, had been a native of Samaria, as was the prophet Samuel. Israel's first king, Saul, along with his sons, were killed in battle on Samaria's Mount Gilboa.

But the united kingdom of Israel had split into northern and southern factions long before there was a Rome to forcibly reunite them. Samaria, the capital of the northern kingdom, often under siege, finally fell to the Assyrians, who carried its leading citizens into exile. The Israelites left behind formed an embattled underclass whose circumstances were further aggravated by the forced settlement of immigrants from other conquered lands among them. When several generations later the exiled Jews were allowed to return to the region, this struggling ethnic minority felt they had suffered the greater persecution—not the privileged class who had actually prospered while in exile. The repatriated aristocrats, on the other hand, were scandalized to see that the Israelites who had been left behind had married some of the foreign settlers.

This ethnic division became so deep that, when Alexander the Great conquered the region, he gave the people of

Samaria permission to build their own temple, one they validated by pointing to a verse in Deuteronomy 27 that named their Mount Ebal as a place of worship. When later the Greeks pressured them politically, however, they allowed the temple to be dedicated to the Greek god Zeus.

Meanwhile, the repatriated southern Jews were faring no better. Their own temple at Jerusalem had been defiled by pagan sacrifice and ritual prostitution. After the Maccabees, the Jewish resistance fighters, led a successful revolt against their foreign oppressors, they reconsecrated their own temple in Jerusalem, but completely destroyed the Samaritans' desecrated temple. Thus, by the time the Romans took over in 65 BC, the Samaritans considered the southern Jews as much their enemy as their pagan conquerors. When the Romans offered Samaritans permission to worship in their own northern way, they eagerly took them up on the offer, thumbing their noses at their sanctimonious southern cousins.

This, then, is the situation Jesus found himself in when he left Jerusalem, headed north toward Galilee and home. While Galileans weren't the pariahs Samaritans were, they were separated from Judea by Samaria and thus geographically isolated from the benefits of solid Jewish teaching and temple culture. Although they had resisted Roman incursion even more stubbornly than the southern Jews, Galileans were looked upon as country bumpkins. So when Jesus—a Galilean—instigated a minor riot in the temple, taking it upon himself to teach them a lesson in religious practices, the Jewish officials did not thank him for pointing out their errors in temple administration. Jesus saw it was time to make himself scarce in the holy city and return to Galilee.

The road north toward home runs through Samaria, but he's in no mood to pay much attention to the travel restrictions set up by the hypocrites hounding him. So, accompanied by his companions, he stops about noon at a town called Sychar, the site of a well dug by the patriarch Jacob over a thousand years earlier. He's hot, tired, and thirsty, yet neither he nor his friends have the necessary equipment for drawing water—a bucket. While his companions go into town to buy food, Jesus approaches a woman who has come to draw water and asks her for a drink.

As soon as he speaks she is on her guard. A man only spoke in public to a strange woman if he believed—or hoped—she wasn't too careful about her reputation. Also, his accent no doubt gives him away. This man, even if only a Galilean, is a Jew. And Jews, she knows, still haven't gotten over that intermarriage issue; they suspect all Samaritans—particularly women—are promiscuous. It's a subject the woman has her own reasons for skirting, so when she answers him, her voice has a defensive edge to it: "What's a Jew like you doing talking to me, a mere Samaritan, and a woman at that? I thought Jews were too good for the likes of us."

Jesus' reply only makes matters worse. "If you only knew who you're talking to," he says, "you'd be asking me for real spring water."

This sounds like an outright insult to the woman. Fine. If that's the way he wants to be, she can go him one better. "Really?" she says. "In case you didn't know, this is a deep well and I don't see any bucket in your hand. Just how do you think you're going to get any water, Mr. High-and-Mighty? But then I guess a Jew like you thinks you're even superior to our forefather Jacob, who provided for his whole family and all his herds from this well."

Again, Jesus' answer sounds to her like typical Jewish bragging. "This? It's just ordinary water. Drink it now and in another hour you'll be thirsty again. But I have some water like you've never tasted before. Just one swallow and you'll never need another drink."

"Well, Mr. Jew," she replies sarcastically, deciding to call his bluff, "let's see this thirst-defying water of yours. It'd sure save me a lot of time and trouble, not having to come to the well anymore."

But this crazy Jew won't back off. "Go get your husband," he urges her. "Then come back."

At once the woman sees she's been outmaneuvered. Just when she thought she'd gotten the upper hand with this guy, trading him taunt for taunt, he outflanks her. All this time he's been sitting there, figuring a way to work marriage into the conversation. Okay. If that's what he wants. "Husband?" she repeats, managing to sound coy and coarse at the same time. "Who said anything about a husband?"

"You've got that right," Jesus answers, quick as lightning, "though that's hardly the whole truth. You've been married five times already. And you're living with a man you're not married to now. At least you told the truth about that."

The woman is shaken by this reply. How did this stranger find out the truth about her? These aren't the kind of wild accusations Jews ordinarily use to stereotype Samaritans— like *half-breed, idol-worshiping whore*. These are just the plain facts about her as an individual.

Thinking quickly, she tries one more time to evade him. The Jews have always made a big deal about the prophets since the Samaritans don't include them in their scripture. She can needle him about that. "So. It looks like I have a prophet on my hands." Her smart-aleck remark sounds uneasy even in her own ears though. Hoping to steer the conversation in a safer direction, she adds, "Tell me something. You Jews say the only proper place to worship is in your city, Jerusalem. But what's wrong with our Mount Ebal? It was good enough for Moses. Why not for you?"

To her surprise, the stranger brushes the question aside. "Jerusalem or Samaria—soon it won't make any difference anyway. There won't be anybody around to worship in either place. It's true—your tradition has been distorted so that you don't have a clear picture of what life's all about, while the Jews have kept their culture intact. But that's really beside the point anyway. Someday—in fact, right now—anyone who truly desires God can worship him. The proper spirit, not the proper place, is all that's required. In fact, God is looking for people who will worship him like that—with their whole hearts."

For some reason, this prospect sounds scarier to the woman than a long lecture on the superiority of Jerusalem to Samaria. That's a battle she's used to fighting. But now she's not sure just where the lines are drawn nor how high the stakes are. "Well," she says tentatively, for the first time trying to establish some common ground between them, "we both believe that there's going to be a final accounting someday when another Anointed One arises to set things straight." Though they disagreed about many things, both the Jews and the Samaritans at least shared this belief—a final, vindicating judgment.

"You're right," Jesus agrees. "And I'm that one, the one both Jews and Samaritans have been waiting for."

But no sooner are these astonishing words out of his mouth than his friends show up. And the woman can see at once that they're not like him. They may not say it, but she can tell what they're thinking—*Why are you wasting your time on her? Don't you know what kind of woman this is?* Before they have a chance to ask the questions openly, she turns on her heel and leaves.

But on the way back to town a sense of wonder grows in her. She figures she knows men pretty well. They hold few surprises for her anymore. After all, she's been through six of them now. But this one—he *is* different. All that business about water that would quench her thirst forever—she'd taken those remarks as insults or showing off. But what if he were serious? Maybe it's been so long since anyone has taken her seriously that she hadn't recognized it when someone did. That last remark about not being married to the man she was living with—that had been the perfect opportunity to call her names, but instead he had put it about as delicately as possible.

However much Jews found fault with them, Samaritans still believed the Messiah would come to see that justice was done—which meant that he'd know the truth about everyone. And he'd certainly had her pegged, all right. But on the other hand, he hadn't been cruel or arrogant about her situation. After all, he would know those divorces weren't *her* doing; Moses had given men the right to cast off their wives, but women had to get by the best way they could. After five times, it just didn't seem worth it to get tied down to a man anymore. Not that there'd been much choice. Being passed around so much had lowered her value; she doubted anyone would marry her now. Yet she needed some kind of protection, some sort of security. Short of being an outright prostitute, this was simply the best deal she'd been able to make. The religious bigwigs—men who looked down on women like her—debated which man she'd belong to in the life to come. Well, if she had anything to say about it, the answer would be none. She'd had enough of this marriage business on earth.

Yet the strange Jew hadn't given her any lectures on morality. All he had done with this mysterious knowledge of his was prove to her that he knew her secrets. He hadn't pointed out all the rules she'd broken. It was the same way he talked about worship regulations—as if the rules, which always ended up favoring the people in charge, weren't really as important as being honest about yourself. Wanting to please God wholeheartedly was what was important, not just making sure you stayed inside the letter of the law.

By the time she reached the town, she'd made up her mind. Nothing like this had ever happened to her before. Nothing like it was likely to happen in the future. She wasn't going to let a little embarrassment stand in the way of a once-in-a-lifetime opportunity. If people in town wanted to make fun of her, she couldn't stop them. But she was going to tell them about this man. She couldn't go too far or they wouldn't believe her. She would only say what she knew for sure—that he'd told her everything she'd done with her life. They would all know what that meant. She'd have to put up with the crude comments, but then she'd plant the question in their minds: Could this clairvoyant be the Messiah? That would get their attention.

It proved to be the perfect ploy. The townspeople flooded through the gates, heading toward the well. "You've got to stay," they insisted after hearing Jesus. "We'll put you up."

And he did. Just like that. For two more days. And ordinarily Jews didn't even eat with Samaritans, much less sleep in their houses. In the end many of them were convinced he was indeed the Messiah they'd been waiting for.

Of course, they were quick to point out to the woman that she shouldn't take credit for that. She only got them interested, whetted their appetites. That was nothing new.

She might have heard though, as she crowded around the well again with the others, the stranger's friends talking about what had happened when they returned from the town. They had brought no one to meet Jesus, of course, just the food they'd bought at the market. Unlike Jesus, they probably wanted to leave Samaria as soon as possible. But instead he had told them to wake up and look around them. This place was ripe for the picking. They ought to get in gear. In a spot like this they could cash in on the work others had already done before they got there, reap the crop someone else had sowed.

Of course, they didn't get it. They hadn't known he was talking about her. She was the one who'd planted the seed, stirred the people up. Or as Saint John Chrysostom would write about her later in his commentary on John: "of her own accord [she] did the work of an evangelist with excited elation."

Women
on the Outside

Ethnic, class, and gender boundaries were clearly drawn in ancient times. A female slave lived within the confines of all three barriers, hardly leaving her room to be human. In the modern world, no single analogue can serve to parallel such an extremely restricted state, though "white slavery" comes close. In countries like Cambodia and Brazil, for instance, young girls, no more than children really, are sometimes sold by their parents to prostitution rings.

The dichotomy between insiders and outsiders deepened for the Israelites after they moved into the Promised Land. Forging a nation from a band of nomads who had only recently been slaves in Egypt required that they develop a corporate identity. This identity was to be based on their worship of a single deity, one who refused all representation in idols and who claimed his realm extended throughout the universe. Such beliefs made the Israelites unique in the region. To protect this identity their laws expressly forbade marriage with Canaanite women who might lead their Hebrew husbands to worship the local gods.

Despite these restrictions, such marriages did occur, however, some crucial to Israel's history. Rahab, from Jericho, was adopted into the tribe and probably married within it. Ruth, from Moab, became the grandmother of Israel's greatest king. On the other hand, Solomon's many foreign wives are credited with undermining the country's religious identity with their importation of their own cults.

Exile in alien lands did not help relax the Jews' attitude

toward outsiders, particularly foreign women. Nor did occupation of their country by the Romans. Jesus recognizes cultural differences and honors historical covenants with his people. Yet he frequently had contact with "foreigners" and left explicit instructions that the message of the Kingdom be spread to "the uttermost part of the earth."[1]

Nor does he allow the boundaries of class or gender to restrict his work. Ignoring religious prohibitions, he associates with social outcasts, both men and women, and touches lepers and other sick people who make him ritually contaminated. Finally, rejected both by his own people and the foreign government, he is himself taken outside the city walls to die.

HAGAR

Genesis 16–17, 21, 25

*A*t first glance, Hagar, the Egyptian slave woman who served as Sarah's handmaid, seems to have absolutely nothing to say to contemporary women. Slavery has been practically abolished from our world. Women, therefore, cannot legally be used in the manner Hagar was. A childless woman, no matter how rich, cannot simply order her husband to impregnate her maid to produce an heir. So while we may experience a momentary shudder at Hagar's situation, we generally think that particular danger is one the civilized world has safely dispensed with.

Think again.

In our recounting of Sarah's story, Hagar appeared only as a secondary character. This time, we recall the story from her point of view.

Hagar has been acquired by the wealthy nomads Abram and Sarai before the Lord changed their names, probably while they were waiting out a famine in Egypt. Very possibly she was part of Pharaoh's deal—along with sheep, cattle, donkeys, camels, and other slaves—to procure Abram's beautiful "sister" Sarai for himself. Hagar must have been a mere child at the time, since, years later when the childless Sarah is seventy-five and her beauty long since faded, Hagar is still young enough to bear a child as her proxy.

Hagar serves Sarai for years as her "maidservant" or "handmaid" (*shifchah* in Hebrew), a status that legally guarantees her protection from both hunger and violence. Evidently, however, sexual barter was not considered violence, despite the fact that, when Sarai finally gives up hope of having a child, Hagar is given no voice in the decision to bear one for her. In fact, the whole idea is Sarai's; even Abram merely assents to and complies with his wife's wishes. Implicit in Sarai's scheme, however, is one often overlooked point in the bargain: "Sarai Abram's wife," the Scripture says, gave Hagar to Abram "to be his *wife*,"[1] using the same word to describe both women. By her own design, Sarai elevates Hagar from the status of maidservant to that of wife. This is a necessary concession if the child who comes from this union is to have the legal status as heir, but also a compromise that will have disastrous consequences. This, however, is the only time in the story that Hagar is called "wife."

This domestic arrangement is evidently short-lived. As soon as Hagar discovers she's pregnant with Abram's child, she despises Sarai—literally, finds her "of lighter weight." Hagar has succeeded where her former mistress has failed. Sarai immediately complains to Abram about Hagar's behavior, calling her maidservant or *shifchah* again instead of wife, and blames him for the unfavorable results of her own scheme. Abram, who never could stand up to the strong Sarai, agrees to Hagar's demotion by referring to her as "maidservant" as well. In fact, he abdicates his involvement in the whole sorry mess. "She's your problem," he says to Sarai. "Deal with it however you want to."

Sarai wastes no time. Scripture uses the same word for her treatment of Hagar that is later used for the Egyptians' treatment of her descendants: she "afflicted," or "humbled," Hagar.

In fact, she mistreats her so badly that, just as the Israelites would later flee from the oppressive Egyptians, Hagar flees from Abram's encampment into the desert, pregnant and alone. No one goes after her. Sarai and Abram seem content to brush the whole affair off as a troublesome incident, a scheme that didn't work.

Someone else has seen her though. As Hagar rests by a spring on the road that runs south back to her Eygptian homeland, a messenger from God speaks to her. As usual, he starts with a question, two actually: "Where have you come from, and where are you going?"[2] (Such messengers, of course, do not really need the information. Just as Jesus frequently asked supplicants, "What do you want?" such questions force those in distress to clarify their desires for themselves, a necessary step for attaining them.)

Hagar has no problem with the first part of the question. "I'm running away from my mistress Sarai,"[3] she replies with admirable frankness. She has nothing to add about where she's going, however. Perhaps for the first time she considers just what might await her in Egypt, should she actually survive the journey alone. Having left there a slave, she would certainly return as one, only now in an even worse predicament—a slave with no owner, no one with even the barest legal obligation to protect or provide for her and her unborn child.

The messenger then supplies her with a plan and a promise. She is to swallow her pride and return to servitude under Sarai—no doubt a galling prospect. And one the messenger might have had difficulty convincing her to adopt, except that he also makes her the kind of offer she can't resist. It is, in fact, the same promise the three strangers will offer her mistress later. Hagar receives it first: her descendants will multiply beyond number. And the slave woman knows that nothing awaiting her in Egypt can compare with that hope.

The messenger goes on to tell her that the child she is carrying is a boy and that she is to name him Ishmael, a word that means "God hears." Thus, though her status of wife or *ishah* has been taken away, *Ishmael* will make up for that loss. In fact, his very name will continually remind Hagar that God heard her desolate, solitary cry in the desert.

The messenger's subsequent description of Ishmael's fate may sound to us like the other shoe dropping, as if, after telling her the good news, he then lays the bad news on her. This son of hers will be a wild man, a fighter, the scourge of the countryside. But Hagar's response to this part of the promise is surprisingly positive. The God-Who-Hears is the name she is to give her son; now she responds by naming God herself— a most unusual occurrence in the Old Testament. She calls him the God-Who-Sees-Me, for just as Moses will, generations later, see "the backside of God" on Mount Sinai, she has, she says, "seen the One who sees me."[4] They have come to an understanding there in the desert, Hagar and God. She has assented to play the part he has written for her in the world's history. They have seen, or as we might say today, "seen into" one another.

Which is why he knew that this slave woman would find the promise of rabble-rousing progeny not a bitter prophecy but a sweet prospect. Briefly elevated to the status of wife, not in order to make more of her but to use her womb as a shortcut to another woman's fulfillment, then plunged into bondage again and abandoned to the spiteful whims of her mistress, Hagar could hardly have desired a child who would suffer the same indignities with docile submission. The news that her descendants would be fighters, terrorizing the very people who had abused her, could only have sounded sweet to Hagar's ears—indeed a vindication. Her enemies had intended not only to use her body to produce a child for themselves; they would have absorbed that very child's identity, thus obliterating hers altogether. She is not sorry to hear that her son will make life rough for them.

Thus, for the sake of her child Hagar returns and submits, as the messenger had instructed her to. And in due time, Ishmael is born. Adding to the sweetness is the fact that, over the years, Abram grows to care deeply for the boy, according him full status as his son. In fact, when this God-Who-Sees makes the name-changing covenant with her child's father, the old man pleads for God's blessing to fall upon his son Ishmael as well. And God again promises to make Hagar's son a father of a great nation, just as her mistress's son will be. In fact, Ishmael is promised twelve sons, each of whom will be ruler of a tribe. And when God establishes circumcision as a sign of the covenant, the thirteen-year-old Ishmael is included—the first bar mitzvah.

Having held off so long in making Sarah a mother, God now delivers on his promise, and her son Isaac is born. This only makes matters worse between the two women, however. Now that Sarah's own son has finally arrived, her determination grows to rid the household of Hagar and Ishmael. On the day the infant Isaac is weaned, Sarah sees the older boy playing with his baby brother. (The word often translated "mocking" in Genesis 21:9 means "laughing" or "playing with"; in fact, it is the same word used in Genesis 21:6 where Sarah describes her laughter at Isaac's birth as well as in earlier chapters to indicate both Sarah and Abraham's reaction to the angel's announcement.) Sarah pounces on the opportunity to complain to Abraham once more. "Get rid of them," she tells her husband. "I don't want that slave's son sharing my boy's inheritance."

Abraham, however, hesitates. Again we see his commitment to his son Ishmael. Only God's reassurance that he will care for Ishmael and deliver on his promise to make the boy the father of a great nation also, allows Abraham to accede once more to Sarah's wishes. So Hagar, who had already lost one home as a slave, is cast out of the only community available to her, the only place that provided her protection. And this because of the jealous resentment of another woman.

The next morning Abraham loads provisions onto Hagar's shoulders and sends her and Ishmael off into the desert. The pair wander there till the water runs out. Then Hagar, in despair, leaves the dehydrated boy in the shade of some bushes and collapses in the sand, far enough away to deaden the sound of her sobbing.

God is still the God-Who-Hears, however. "What's wrong, Hagar?" he asks. "Don't be afraid. I hear your son's cries. Get up. Get your boy to his feet. I'm still determined to make him a nation." And he points her in the direction of an oasis that, till then, she hadn't noticed in the desert wilderness. Thus, she and Ishmael are saved.

Instead of striking out for Egypt as she had when she ran away earlier, Hagar remains in the desert. God, we are told, also remains with them there as she raises her son in the Wilderness of Paran, the same desolate country where the descendants of her rival Sarah will one day wander themselves. When Ishmael is of an age to marry, Hagar selects his wife for him, an Egyptian like herself. Hagar's grandchildren become nomads like their grandfather Abraham, hardy hunters and fierce warriors able to thrive in the harsh terrain of northern Arabia.

Obviously Abraham continues to recognize Hagar's son as his own, even though Isaac inherits his wealth, because the last we see of Ishmael, he and his younger brother are burying their father Abraham in a cave. The fortunes of the two boys remain intertwined. Ironically, Isaac, Sarah's son, ends up living by the very well where Hagar had first met God, the one she named "The Well of the One Who Sees Me" so many years before. And Muslims today claim that Mohammed, founder of Islam, was a direct descendant of Hagar and Abraham through Ishmael. If so, we see fulfillment of God's promise to Hagar and her progeny on three continents.

But if the fate of Isaac and Ishmael were intertwined, tragic strands of which reach into our own history today, it was only because their mothers' lives were knotted into snarls of envy and suspicion. In a day when nurture and empathy are claimed as almost exclusively the province of women, the relationship between Hagar and Sarah provides a corrective to that facile oversimplification. Sarah, who knew what it felt like to be sexually bartered, nevertheless gives her maid to her husband as a surrogate womb. Though some might argue that this was a career move upward for Hagar the slave, one she would not have protested herself, such reasoning is like defending baby farming among poor women on the grounds that renting their wombs would allow them to raise their standard of living. Whatever gratification either Sarah or Hagar might have hoped for was canceled by this demeaning use of the body. This is not the only account of surrogate motherhood in the Bible. Both Leah and Rachel give their maids to their husband Jacob to impregnate. As with Sarah and Hagar, this act is motivated by envy and quickly degenerates into a kind of fertility competition. The resulting children are infected by their mothers' spirit of envy and suspicion, then eventually sell their half-brother Joseph to slave traders.

The Bible neither praises nor encourages women's contending with one another for male favors. Even the supposed winners in these competitions ultimately endure suffering they could not have imagined at the height of their victory over their rivals.

Sarah no doubt gloated as Hagar was driven into the wilderness with her child and only as much food and water as she could carry, but her day of reckoning came soon. In the chapter following Hagar's banishment is the story of Abraham taking Isaac to sacrifice him on Mount Moriah. Since the account is told from Abraham's point of view, we don't know if Sarah even knew what her husband was up to when he set out with her only child, the son she had waited for so long, the wood for his own immolation bound to the back of the donkey trailing after him. Did she ever learn the truth about this trip? Did Isaac tell her how he had watched his father raise the knife, ready to plunge it into him?

If so, maybe then she remembered Hagar.

SYRO-PHOENICIAN WOMAN

Matthew 15:21-28, Mark 7:24-30

*D*uring Roman times, the district of Galilee was the last northern outpost of Judaism, cut off from the holy city of Jerusalem with its temple by the region of Samaria. Beyond Galilee lay Syria, a stretch of coastland settled in past ages by the seafaring Phoenicians. To this region, homeland of Israel's ancient enemies, Jesus retreats with his disciples. They have recently been under attack from the Pharisees for failing to observe certain hand-washing rituals. Needing a break from these extended and heated controversies, they find a safe haven in the coastal city of Tyre.

Because Jesus hopes to remain incognito while there, he stays indoors so that he won't be recognized and thus draw the crowds that inevitably congregate around him. Nevertheless, a native of the region, a Greek woman, discovers his presence in the community and slips into the house. She's not there to get his autograph though. She has an urgent request: a demon possesses her daughter and she wants Jesus to get rid of it.

As supplicants often did, she falls at his feet to make her appeal. Jesus ignores her.

This response—or, as Matthew records the story, failure to respond—shocks us. Nowhere else in the gospels does Jesus display such seeming indifference and lack of compassion toward a petitioner. The Jesus we know and love never turns anyone away. Yet this woman he ignores. Nevertheless, she continues to cry out to him to have mercy and heal her daughter. Such a ruckus does she raise that the disciples, realizing her shouts will soon draw a crowd, plead with Jesus to get rid of her, send her away, do something to shut her up.

To that end, Jesus turns to her and delivers the cruelest words recorded as coming from his mouth. "I'm not here on your account," he tells her. "I'm here to help my own people who are in bad shape. They're lost and wandering. I can't waste my time and energy on you. That would be like taking food out of the children's mouth and giving it to the puppies under the table." (The Greek word is not "dogs" but "puppies," the only softened note in this harsh refusal.)

Many layers of history and culture lie beneath this apparently heartless reply. Mark's description of the woman emphasizes that she is Greek both by birth and religion. Yet she is not the first non-Jew to beg for Jesus' help. Already he has healed the Roman centurion's slave. But that was back in the Jewish province of Galilee, and the centurion, recognizing his delicate position as an outsider, demonstrated a sensitivity to Jewish religious tradition by forbearing to ask Jesus to come to his Gentile home.

Here in Syria, however, Jesus and his band are on alien soil, no longer surrounded by monotheistic Jews who automatically connect morality with deity. Tyre was a pagan city; its citizens would only understand this healer as one of many itinerant wonder-workers, more on the order of a magician than a holy man. For the Greeks, and indeed for most of the Middle Eastern peoples, healing had no necessary connection to holiness. Exorcism in particular was the special province of magicians. In their eyes, supernatural powers could only be manipulated by sorcerers adept in occult skills.

A similar scene in Acts 16 shows how this form of pagan spiritualism operated. Luke reports that, while he and the Apostle Paul are in Philippi, the largest city in Macedonia, a slave girl whose owners used her commercially as a fortuneteller frequently followed them, calling out loudly that they were "servants of the Most High God."[1] (In the Bible, spirits, even evil ones, appear compelled to publicly recognize emissaries of God.) Modern spiritualism would call the slave girl a "medium," meaning her consciousness could at times be taken over by a spirit who could link her up with the underworld—using her as a kind of spiritual communication modem. When Paul and Silas free her from this possession and restore her to her right mind, they are taken to court by the girl's owners. Such occult practicioners were so much a part of the life of the times that they were a recognized service industry. Paul and Silas lose the case, are flogged, and put in prison for depriving the plaintiffs of their legal livelihood.

In Jewish territories, however, such practices were forbidden. Of all the ancient peoples of the Middle East, only the Jews had any inkling that power to command demons came only from the one God who created the universe and everything in it, who maintained it by his power, a power that was not for sale, could not be used for commercial purposes, or otherwise exploited for selfish human ends.

Thus, when the Syro-Phoenician woman entreats Jesus to exorcise the demon in her daughter, he realizes how little she understands her own request. If Jesus indulges the woman's request too easily, he could in fact feed her superstitious illusions and lead her further into the realm of darkness where she would remain prey to fear of demonic powers. Nothing, in the end, would be accomplished. Unless she recognizes the source of Jesus' power, both she and her daughter will continue to live at the mercy of dark forces beyond their control.

Earlier in Matthew Jesus has already told those who wanted to see him put on a magic show that exorcising demons from people of such shallow understanding does no good. Even if the first unclean spirit leaves them, they will soon be reinfested sevenfold.

The woman remains insistent, however. Instead of leaving in a huff at the unflattering comparison Jesus has just made, she assures him that she takes his point about feeding children before puppies. "True enough," she agrees, "yet even the puppies are allowed to scavenge the crumbs that fall from the table."

This retort acknowledges that there is indeed an essential difference between the religion of pagans and that of Jews. Something more than cultural diversity is at stake. Pagan understanding of supernatural power is stunted and incomplete. Magic is not the same as miracle. Connecting wholeness and holiness is crucial. Her reply shows Jesus that she perceives a difference between her own background of occultism and his tradition of righteousness. Nevertheless, she is willing to be fed, if only by the crumbs of that tradition, knowing that her people's gods offer her neither healing nor protection. With great humility, she acknowledges her position as an outsider, someone who does not fully understand, a person to whom, after a certain amount of religious instruction, the Jews might award the title "God-fearer"— though they would never admit her to the inner court of their temple.

At that point, Jesus eagerly responds to her request. He does not wait till her understanding is full and complete— after all, his own inner circle frequently demonstrate their deplorable ignorance about his mission. Her simple confession that she'd rather feed on the crumbs of reality than starve on illusions is enough for Jesus. In fact, it carries sufficient weight for him to declare her faith great.

Indeed, it looks a good deal sturdier than that of the Pharisees Jesus has come to her city to escape. While she is willing to gather up the crumbs under the table of Jewish tradition, they, the very teachers and most impeccable practitioners of that tradition, have lost sight of its purpose—the healing of nations. Just as healing cannot occur without holiness, holiness that's lost its mission is hollow. The embryonic faith of this foreign woman, therefore, offers an opening for grace, while their strict but sterile observances block its power. The Pharisees, had they been there, would have considered the woman unclean. But while they worry about washing their hands, the woman has salvaged her whole child.

It is interesting that, when Jesus leaves Tyre, he immediately returns to his work along the Sea of Galilee, feeding four thousand people who have brought their sick friends and relatives for him to heal. Afterward, he has his disciples gather up the leftover bits of broken bread and fish. No doubt the Phoenician woman's remark about the crumbs that fall from the table still echoed in his mind.

The story of the Syro-Phoenician woman, oddly enough, does not appear in the Gospel of Luke, which makes a point of including both Gentiles and women in its narrative. Luke, however, does recount the parable of the importunate widow, whose point, he says, is that we should always "pray and not lose heart."[2] The setting for the parable is an unnamed "certain town," and the characters are the judge who neither fears God nor cares about man, and the widow who pleads relentlessly with him till he grants her request. Jesus ends the parable, "Will not God bring about justice for his chosen ones, who cry out to him day and night? Will he keep putting them off? I tell you, he will see that they get justice, and quickly."[3]

Perhaps he was remembering again that foreign woman who had cried out to him and refused to be silent, grasping for the crumbs to feed herself and heal her daughter.

WOMAN WITH
THE ISSUE OF BLOOD

Matthew 9:20-22, Mark 5:24-34, Luke 8:43-48;
see also Leviticus 15

*N*othing in women's lives makes them universally feel their peculiarity so much as menstruation. Practically all cultures have some kind of ceremony to mark for girls the beginning of this monthly bleeding. These initiation ceremonies not only put the community members on notice that the girl is no longer a child but is a woman capable of bearing children, but also impress on the girl that menstruation changes her life forever in definitive, irrevocable ways.

Less technological societies often isolate menstruating women from the general community as well. Blood, especially our own, unnerves us. The bright red stain, the sensation of constant seeping, even the fetid smell of oxidizing hemoglobin assault the senses, shaming women into concealing this physical condition they find themselves in a good percentage of their lifetimes.

Women in technological societies feel a certain loss of control during menstruation, as raw nature asserts itself within our antiseptic environment. Despite the way sex education has alleviated certain fears and misunderstandings, despite frank public advertisements about "feminine hygiene products," we still don't feel the same about this physiological process as we do about, say, the buildup of dental plaque. There are women who purport to enjoy pregnancy; I have never met a woman who actually *enjoys* menstruating. And to bleed constantly from some inner wound for twelve years— the notion appalls us. Yet such was the condition of the woman described by the gospel writers as having "an issue of blood."[1]

Jews had regulations governing menstruating women's access to public places as well as directions about what we consider private matters—sexual relations with husbands during this period. The twelfth and fifteenth chapters of Leviticus deal specifically with these regulations, though the Jews were not unique in imposing such restrictions on women. Similar regulations limited menstruating women's access to the temples of the goddess Artemis, for example.

A woman was called "unclean" or "impure"[2] by Jewish law during her period, and though these terms were used only in a ritual context and did not necessarily connote dirtiness or sinfulness, a woman's sense of herself could not have been unaffected by the label. The rules governing menstruating women are the same as those for any community member with some sort of fluid discharge from the body (including semen). Not only did Jewish law exclude such people from the temple; other members of their community were not to touch them, sit in a chair they had occupied, or touch any items they might have handled. After the discharge stopped, the regulations required a ritual bath, or baptism, to prepare the person for return to activity in the community.

But what if the discharge doesn't stop? What if it goes on, day after day, week after week, even year after year? For one thing, one becomes anemic from constant blood loss. But that's only the physiological effect. Socially there are problems as well. Nonstop bleeding inhibits one's activities in public, makes working difficult, demands extraordinary hygienic precautions. The physical dysfunction is emotionally draining as well. The nagging sense of being out of tune with normal body cycles affects one's whole sense of self; the sufferer feels out of sync with the cosmos. And finally, there's the financial depletion from protracted medical attention.

Such was the state of the woman described in the gospels as having "an issue of blood." It's not an uncommon physical condition even today, and two thousand years of changing cultural patterns and medical progress have not altered the basic elements of this predicament. Nevertheless, she would have had to live isolated from the rest of the community during the twelve years she endured this condition. Those touching her or any of her belongings would have been considered contaminated themselves. If she were married, it would mean the end of that relationship. Friends or family could conceivably have helped her, but the constant purification ritual needed to cleanse themselves after contact with her would become a tiresome chore after a while. Though sick people were sometimes brought to Jesus by their friends or family, they usually suffered from fever or were lame or blind, not conditions that isolated the sufferer as hers did.

The Gospel of Mark provides by far the fullest account of this woman's story, though none of the versions provide her with a name. She is simply one of the nameless figures in the crowd pushing to get close to Jesus as he steps off a boat that has just brought him across the Sea of Galilee.

So famous has Jesus already become as a healer that it's all his disciples can do to keep the waiting crowds from mobbing him. A woman—an anemic one at that—didn't stand much chance in that crowd. And, in fact, someone else gets to Jesus first. An important synagogue official, someone people make way for. And, unlike the woman, he has a name—Jairus. It was probably in his own synagogue at Capernaum that a man had earlier been dispossessed of the "unclean spirit" that tormented him. At any rate, the crowd parts so that he can approach Jesus and ask him to come to his house where his twelve-year-old daughter lies near death.

The woman may have once been wealthy herself, since she has spent all her money on a variety of doctors. In fact, Mark says she has "suffered"[3] under their care, is now penniless, and all to no avail. Instead of getting better, her condition has steadily worsened. Jesus is her last hope of health. She seizes this opportunity, the lull in the crowd's clamor as Jesus stands listening to Jairus' request, to slip closer to the healer. She has no reason to believe that he would talk to her the way he's talking to Jairus. She knows she is an untouchable. The occasion calls for stealth.

We have no information as to what had convinced her that a mere touch, without even his knowledge, would be enough to heal her. Had she seen him heal others in Capernaum? Had she been friends with Peter's mother-in-law, whose fever had been chased away so easily by her son-in-law's friend? Maybe she'd heard the leper who, despite Jesus' request for anonymity, had babbled for days about the man who'd healed him. Perhaps the similarity of their positions as untouchables had first put the idea into her head. If Jesus had healed a leper and if the priest had given him a clean bill of health, maybe there was hope for her too.

At any rate, while everyone else's attention is focused on the two men who are already moving off toward Jairus' house, and convinced she will never come any closer to the healer, the woman reaches out and touches Jesus' clothes. No sooner have her fingers grazed the fabric than she feels the blood cease to flow from her body.

Jesus stops in the middle of the road, people jamming up against him. "Who did that?" he demands, looking around. "Who touched me?"[4]

His companions shake their heads. "What do you mean?" they ask impatiently. "Here we are, about to be trampled by this mob, and you want to know who touched you?" Neither they nor we understand the mechanics of how this healing power works. Just as the woman immediately feels in her body that she is healed, so Jesus knows in himself that power has gone out of him. From his disciples' remark it's clear other people were jostling him, very possibly wanting some miracle themselves. But only this woman's touch called forth Jesus' healing power.

The woman is understandably afraid. She knows this man has every right to be angry since she has defiled him. Expecting a rebuke, she falls down before him, confessing what she has done as if it were a crime, expecting his anger.

Instead, his response is unexpectedly gentle. His first word to her is "Daughter."[5] This, to one to whom every human contact has, for twelve long years, been denied. The very word must be like balm to her terror, implying as it does not merely connection but protection. In one word Jesus reassures her that her infraction of the regulations will bring her no harm. At the same time, however, he doesn't patronize her by saying, "I know you're a poor, sick woman, desperate enough to try anything. And I'm overlooking this incident, but next time, make an appointment." (One of the most appealing characteristics of Jesus is the way he dealt with individuals immediately. He never had scheduling problems or an appointment calendar.)

Instead, he applauds rather than condemns her audacity: "It's your faith that's healed you," he tells her. If she hadn't been willing to relinquish what little dignity she had left, she might never have been whole again. If she hadn't put aside her fear of embarrassment and exposure, she could not receive the peace he now bestows on her as a blessing. That's why this woman's touch is different from the others'. Undoubtedly many in the crowd wanted to be healed, but she was the one who had something at risk.

Living faith—the kind that calls forth a response—stakes its life on the answer. When we approach God, however hesitantly, we are always teetering on the margin of life whether we recognize it or not. Faith never comes alive except on the edge. Hedging one's bets is not the same as having faith. An instructive contrast to this woman is Nicodemus, a wealthy, well-educated man who, despite his protected position, nevertheless comes to Jesus by night rather than in the press of the crowd. What he wanted from Jesus was philosophical discussion. Perhaps Jesus' use of a physiological metaphor—being born again—was chosen in order to show Nicodemus how much was at stake, that faith is a life-and-death matter.

The lap of luxury stifles faith; emotional self-sufficiency smothers it. That's why it's always the marginal people Jesus notices. Not only this woman but the widow who put her two pennies—all she had—into the temple treasury. If the woman with the issue of blood had not already spent all her money on doctors, she might still have clung to the hope that they could cure her. The end of our rope is where we're always closest to God.

Single Women

In the Old Testament, single women are notable by their absence. Although widows made up such a significant portion of the population that a number of laws in Deuteronomy provide for their special protection and the prophets frequently mention their mistreatment as examples of Israel's sin, women who never married are few and far between.

Given the economic structure of the Old Testament world, which, even during the high point of the Jerusalem monarchy, remained 90 percent agricultural, it is easy to see how singleness was neither a value nor an option for women. Farm labor in Palestine was home-grown; producing not only heirs but workers was a large part of women's contribution to the economy. Single women could not supply the muscle-power for clearing, plowing, planting, and harvesting necessary to agriculture in the rocky Palestinian plains. And, given the polygamy inherited from their nomadic ancestors, no woman had to be excluded from some sort of position within a household, even if it were only as a second or third wife or a concubine.

Thus marriage was an economic necessity, and daughters a marketable commodity. Since marrying Canaanite women was expressly forbidden (though, of course, this proscription was not strictly followed), daughters could bring their families a considerable "bride-price." Marriage then benefited the whole community and was an essential component of its agricultural economy.

During New Testament times, however, when urban life

with its market economy grew stronger, staying single or not remarrying if widowed became an option. The difference between the agricultural world of the Old Testament and the urban world of the New Testament shows up in women's attitudes toward producing children. For all the healing done by Jesus, no woman ever approaches him for a fertility cure as Sarah and Hannah besought God in the Old Testament. A woman's value was no longer tied solely to reproduction as it had been in the earlier agricultural period. Women could own and operate their own business, like Lydia of Philippi, or maintain a household, like Mary and Martha, without being married.

In fact, during the apostolic period, singleness, for the first time in scriptural history, actually became an honored state, advocated by Paul as the preferred condition for those serious about their work for the Lord. Single people, he points out, are unencumbered by marital duties and thus undistracted from their devotion to Christ. (Of course, he also assumes that celibacy will accompany singleness.) Such a position would have been unthinkable, especially for women, in earlier times.

MARTHA

Luke 10:38-42; John 11:1-46, 12:1-2

*L*uke gives us our earliest view of Martha of
Bethany. In a deceptively simple domestic scene,
one that sets the tone for the later episodes, we
see Martha preparing a meal in her home. We're not sure if
she knew Jesus before he decided to stop over at her house in
a suburb of Jerusalem, or if he merely showed up in Bethany
and waited for someone to invite him to supper. Earlier in the
same chapter Jesus had directed seventy-two of his followers to go ahead of him into all the towns he expected to visit,
instructing them to take no provisions but instead to depend
on the hospitality they encountered there. However poor such
accommodations might prove, the disciples were not to criticize but to eat what was set before them.

So perhaps this advance team had already made arrangements with Martha for Jesus' arrival—along with his twelve
disciples, an important detail in the story that is often overlooked. No wonder Martha is nervous about dinner preparations; she'll have at least thirteen guests at her table tonight.

And it *is* her table. Though she has a sister, Mary, and a

brother, Lazarus, the story emphasizes that the house belongs to Martha. (See Mary's story, pages 143-146.) There's a possibility that she was a widow, but Luke, who frequently uses that term to identify other women in his narrative, does not classify Martha as one. Nor is she called "the wife of" or even "the daughter of," the ancient world's way of providing women with a last name. In this first encounter with Jesus, even Lazarus, the brother of these women, is not mentioned, possibly an indication he is a good bit younger than the two sisters. Thus the strongest probability is that Martha was a single woman, as was her sister Mary.

As to Martha's social position, it's hard to know how much to make of the fact that Martha's name means "lady," the feminine form of "lord" in Hebrew. Nevertheless, whether because of inheritance or her own business acumen, Martha is well off enough to own her own home. And socially sensitive enough to be concerned about hosting such a notable guest as Jesus. On the other hand, she is not so wealthy that she can simply leave all the dinner preparations to servants. Indeed, this fact occasions the conflict in the story. While Martha is bustling about in the kitchen, her sister Mary is ignoring her responsibilities and sitting in the living room, absorbed in the "man-talk" of Jesus and his followers.

Slaving over a hot stove in the kitchen while others are enjoying themselves is guaranteed to put anyone out of sorts. "Distracted"[1] is the way the *New International Version* describes Martha's mental and emotional state. The *King James Version* says she was "cumbered."[2] The Greek verb only occurs this once in the New Testament and means literally "to draw around." Martha has drawn around her like a barricade the complications that automatically attend a large dinner party. Paradoxically, this screens her off as well from the *pièce de résistance* of the evening, Jesus himself. Finally, flushed and frustrated with too much to do and too little help, Martha flounces into the living room and makes a scene, complaining to the very guest she is purposing to honor about her sister's behavior.

Which is precisely what she needed to do.

Martha's social *faux pas*, her plaintive wail, cracks the otherwise smooth surface of the evening, and out of that crack comes boiling the volcanic truth of Martha's soul—resentment and a feeling of abandonment. "Lord, don't you care?" she cries. "Mary's not helping at all. I'm having to do all the work by myself. Tell her she has to help me." The words burst from her with the injured tone of a child protesting cosmic injustice. *It isn't fair! It isn't fair!*

Every woman in the world has felt like Martha. (Which is why countless Sunday school classes and women's circles are named after her.) And not just while slaving over a hot stove listening to other people laughing and talking in the living room. We feel like this when left alone with the laundry while everyone else goes off to work or to class where work is recognized and appreciated. At home, no one rewards you with money or grades for the drudgery you do. You clock long years of child rearing, and later, of being tied down by aging or sick parents—all the jobs that have to be done but never get noticed. Jobs everyone else in the world seems to successfully avoid—except you.

It's bad enough that husbands, sons, fathers, brothers manage to opt out of those responsibilities—but another woman? Your own sister? Who does she think she is, anyway? Thus is Martha—thus are we all—reduced to childish, impotent rage at the overwhelming inequity of our unacknowledged lives spent in unappreciated labor. Doesn't anybody care?

Martha's indignation is honest, straight from the bottom of her soul, and that's why it was right. Much better to say straight out to Jesus what's on your mind than to take the more devious approach, the one that says, "Oh no. Never mind. I'm fine. Go ahead and have a good time. Don't worry about me."

Throughout the gospels Jesus constantly asks people, "What do you want?" or "What do you want me to do for you?" And as long as people tell him frankly the desire of their heart, they get it. In Martha's situation, however, Jesus can't give her precisely what she asks for without taking it away from someone else, in this case, her sister. Nevertheless, he hears the deepest stratum of her bitterness: "Don't you care?" *Don't I matter too?*

And in this complex narrative, compressed into a mere five sentences, Luke expends two words to have Jesus repeat her name as a prelude to his response—"Martha, Martha."[3] Though Luke wastes no adjectives describing his tone of voice, in the very repetition of her name we hear the nuances. Since she has spoken as a child, Jesus calms the child in her. Simultaneously, however, the very naming affirms her significance. To him she is not an unimportant kitchen flunky but an individual.

But we also catch a tone of regret, even see him shake his head slightly. He will not grant the more overt part of her request—that he order her sister into the kitchen also. Misery may love company, but one injustice cannot be assuaged by inflicting another. Instead, he describes to Martha her current condition: "You're upset and distracted by details." Then he tells her the hard truth: "But only one thing is actually necessary. Mary has chosen that. And it won't be taken from her."

There's much to be unpacked from this response. Note, for one thing, that Martha's distraction really is with the superfluities of social life, not inescapably essential domestic chores. Jesus doesn't trivialize domestic duties by brushing them aside as insignificant. Martha, after all, is not changing diapers or doing the weekly laundry.

The two sisters have been given what both must have seen as a remarkable opportunity—having this great teacher as a guest in their home. How they decide to take advantage of that opportunity is their own choice. Do they spend the time putting on a big spread or do they use it listening to what he has to say? A man who's just sent seventy-two people out into the countryside with only the cloaks on their backs is hardly going to encourage his other supporters to dither over social superfluities. He's only moving his Sermon on the

Mount indoors here, telling Martha to consider the lilies of the field. Anxiety about what to eat or drink is a problem for women as well as men—maybe more so. But it's a predicament he's offering to free Martha from.

The trick, however, is that the freedom has to be chosen. One has to deliberately embrace the one necessary thing instead of the many distracting things. Mary, he says, *chose* the better part. It was not a role assigned to her by her culture, certainly. Her very presence there in the living room among the male disciples no doubt occasioned a few raised eyebrows. Nevertheless, having chosen, she cannot have it taken away. Not to placate public perceptions of what is seemly; not even to assuage the private feelings of her sister.

It is interesting that Luke tells this story from Martha's point of view. Mary never speaks or acts in the whole scene. Was she aware of her sister's distress? Was she embarrassed by her outburst? We don't know. Just as we don't know how Martha reacted to Jesus' response.

We do know, however, that the friendship between the great man and the two women of Bethany continued, because they reappear in his story some time later at what was a critical point in all their lives. The Jerusalem religious establishment has sought to end increasingly bitter controversies by attempting to take Jesus into custody. Jesus then retreats from Judea to the far side of the Jordan, the site of his baptism where his ministry began. Even there, however, he continues to draw large crowds.

While there, he receives word from the two sisters that their brother Lazarus is sick. It is a simple message, emphasizing the bond between the two men; it does not request that Jesus leave his safe haven to come and heal their brother. Though they no doubt wish this were possible, the two women refrain from making the request explicit since they know a return to Bethany—less than two miles from Jerusalem— would expose Jesus to grave danger, a fact that's often been overlooked in dealing with this story.

And indeed, Jesus makes no move to return. His remark—
"This sickness is not unto death"[4]—the disciples no doubt
took at the time to mean that Lazarus' illness would not prove
fatal. But lest we think his remark unfeeling, the gospel repeats
for emphasis the fact that Jesus "loved Martha, her sister, and
Lazarus,"[5] again naming Martha first as though she is the
acknowledged head of the household.

Finally, after two days, Jesus announces to his disciples
that they're heading back to Judea. His companions are aghast.
"You're going back? But they just tried to stone you there!"
Jesus, however, is determined, and subtly reminds them of
their own obligation to the Bethany family by calling Lazarus
"*our* friend"[6] whom he knows has already died. As Jesus
and his band near Bethany, they hear that Lazarus was indeed
buried four days ago.

Meanwhile, Jews from Jerusalem have come to Bethany
to join Martha and Mary in the customary Jewish mourning
ceremonies, which last for a full week. When Martha hears
that Jesus is coming, she slips out of the house and goes to
intercept him, leaving the guests to Mary this time—the guests
who surely pose a threat to her friend. Her emotions are mixed,
to say the least, when she sees him. While fearing for his safety,
she's also still grieving for her brother, so a slight reproach
colors her greeting to Jesus: "This wouldn't have happened if
you had been here." Then she adds, with a surge of hope, "But
you can still fix it. God always listens to you and does what
you ask."

Jesus replies matter-of-factly, "Your brother will rise
again."[7]

No doubt Martha, always conventional herself, hears this
as one of those rote phrases by which we offer one another
condolences. As if reciting a catechism, she parrots back to
him the accepted Jewish belief in a general resurrection at the
end of time. But we can hear the disappointment in her voice.
A catechism is cold comfort at this moment, though it looks
as if that's all she's likely to get from Jesus.

"No," he says. "You don't understand. *I* am the resurrection and the life. If you believe that, it doesn't matter if he's dead. He'll live again."

"Okay, okay," she replies. She's never been particularly interested in theological discussions and certainly doesn't have time for one now. "I know. You're the Messiah, the one we've been waiting for to come into the world." Within, however, she's probably thinking, *But what good has that done me? My brother's dead now. I don't want to have to wait till the end of time to see him again.*

Then she hurries away, leaving him there in the graveyard, and goes home to get her sister who will no doubt get more out of all this religious talk than she has.

Back at the house, she must be cautious because the Jerusalem Jews are still there. She tells Mary secretly about Jesus' arrival, adding—a kind touch—that the rabbi is calling for her in particular.

Overcome by excitement, Mary recklessly rushes out of the house and up the road to the cemetery. When she sees Jesus, she falls at his feet. She may have more of an intellectual bent than her older sister, but her feelings at the moment mirror Martha's; thus her first words are similar. "If you had been here, this would never have happened. Lazarus wouldn't have died." Like her sister, she has enough faith to believe Jesus can stave off death by healing people. But bring them back to life again? All well-informed Jews knew the soul only lingers in the vicinity of the body for three days, during which a healer might manage a miraculous restoration. But after four days, all hope has to be abandoned.

Mary has been so reckless in running from the house to see Jesus, however, that the entire mourning party has noticed and followed her. Before the two friends know it they are surrounded by suspicious Jerusalemites. Jesus looks around distressed. The word used here to describe his reaction has been variously translated as "groaned inwardly," "was deeply moved," and "was angry." Except for this story, the Greek verb is used nowhere else in the New Testament, though the Greek playwright Aeschylus employed it to describe the snorting of horses. Certainly, the word betokens intense emotional expression and is coupled in the sentence with "troubled." Does it mean Jesus was distressed at his friends' lack of faith or understanding? Was he upset by the sudden appearance of his enemies? Or was he overwhelmed by his own sorrow at Lazarus' death?

He raises his voice over the wails of the mourners and merely asks, "Where have you buried him?" When they point out the tomb, a limestone cave sealed up with a stone in the same fashion his own would shortly be, Jesus begins to weep as well.

This time the gospel puts our questions about the specific reason for this display of emotion into the mouths of the bystanders. Some say he is mourning for his well-loved friend; others think these are tears of self-reproach for not having come soon enough to heal Lazarus of the fatal illness. Instead of confirming either of these speculations, the gospel once more says that Jesus "snorted." "Remove the stone," he commands.[8]

Martha, practical to the point of bluntness, protests: "But he'll stink by now!"

"Didn't I tell you that if you'd believe you'd see God's glory?" Jesus asks.

By now the others have wrestled the stone from the entrance to the cave. The people crowding around are holding their collective breath. But Jesus pauses, then begins to speak, addressing his words skyward: "Father, I give you thanks for hearing me. I know you always hear me, but I'm saying this aloud for the sake of those standing around here so that they can believe that you've sent me." No doubt he particularly had Martha in mind. Jesus has known since he received word of Lazarus' illness on the far side of the Jordan four days and many miles ago that he would restore his friend to life, give him back to his sisters. What distresses Jesus is the unnecessary heartache these friends, the ones who know him best, still insist on inflicting on themselves. It all seems so simple to him. Yet no amount of teaching seems to penetrate their understanding. Whether it's dinner or death makes little difference; they're always worried about the wrong thing.

Jesus takes a deep breath. "Lazarus," he cries. "Come out!"

And out of the mouth of the cave shuffles the startling figure of Lazarus, still wrapped mummylike in strips of linen burial bandages. The sight had to be at once astonishing and appalling, like a scene from a horror movie. Everyone is so immobilized, both with hope and with dread of walking corpses, that Jesus has to tell them to unwind the bandages and free Lazarus.

In her jubilation over her brother's restoration, Martha decides to throw another dinner party. The gospel once again puts Martha in the kitchen, just as she was before, slaving over the hot stove. This time, however, without protest. Perhaps because she's so filled with gratitude that she needs the outlet of physical activity to express it. But also she now sees that this is work, not imposed, but freely chosen. Her own last supper with her Lord is her gift, not her duty.

In Catholic and Orthodox traditions, the sisters Martha and Mary have been emblematic of the two different spiritual paths. Martha is the active "server." That Greek verb—from which our word "deacon" derives—is always attached to her in the Bible. Martha expresses her devotion through physical action. Too often, however, her service has been interpreted as that of someone who hovers in the background, patient and practically invisible. But when we look at her story, we find that Martha's serving does not make her less assertive. She speaks up, forges ahead, takes charge. As head of her household, she doesn't hesitate to cause a scene at a dinner party. She's the one who hurries out to intercept Jesus when he returns to Bethany and who tries to keep his presence secret from his enemies. She even argues with Jesus about opening her brother's tomb. Martha is not a follower, but a leader.

Whether active or contemplative, both these women had to be single for this story to happen, given the cultural climate of the times. Only as head of her household would Martha have had the effrontery to burst into the living room with her complaint. Not she but her husband would have gone out to meet Jesus at her brother's tomb. Married, Mary would not have sat at Jesus' feet but only heard his words secondhand.

Women with husbands and children cannot reasonably expect to fulfill the duties that come with the life they've chosen and also throw themselves wholeheartedly into a cause or work night and day. When marriage fuses the very flesh of two people, it merges their time and energy as well. Schedules have to be coordinated, work organized, behavior moderated. All action is undertaken knowing it affects another person.

Martha could both serve and speak up precisely because she was single. There are some freedoms only bestowed on the single state.

JEPHTHAH'S DAUGHTER

Judges 11

*I*n an age when women were routinely raped during war and either slaughtered or taken as the spoils of victory, the story of Jephthah's daughter chills the reader more than these more passionate forms of violence. This tale takes a relationship that should provide protection for the weak and turns it upside down, so that the natural protector—in this case a father—becomes the aggressor. It underscores the terrifying fact of the single woman's vulnerability.

The story begins, as most family sagas do, with a previous generation, Jephthah's own parents. His father had been a man of means in Gilead, a town that repeatedly had turned to the cultic practices of their pagan neighbors, including the Ammonites. Sharing their gods did not, however, offer the Israelites any protection from these warlike peoples, and the city was often besieged.

Jephthah himself was the product of his father's own infidelity with a foreign prostitute, a physical analogue to the Israelites' spiritual fascination with alien gods. Jephthah's brothers—all of them the sons of the father's legal wives—ran their bastard brother out of town when they began to fear he might demand a share in the family inheritance. Having already established a reputation as "a mighty man of valor," Jephthah, after his banishment, gathered a gang of desperadoes about him, holing up in a place called, no doubt with irony, Tov—the Land of Good.

When next the Ammonites attack Gilead, the elders of the city send to the bandit chief asking for his help. Understandably, Jephthah is reluctant to ride to the rescue of the town that's turned its back on him. He only consents to help when they promise that, if he defeats the Ammonites, the elders will make him head of the city council.

After lengthy and futile diplomatic negotiations with the Ammonites, Jephthah prepares for war. Marching toward the enemy encampment, he pauses before going into battle to make a final vow: if the Lord delivers his enemies into his hands, he will offer as a sacrifice the first thing that comes out of the door to meet him when he returns home victorious. It is important to note here that the Lord neither asks for nor acknowledges this vow. Indeed, it is the kind of vow, offering a possible human sacrifice, that a pagan warrior might have made.

Nevertheless, Jephthah is successful, reclaiming twenty towns and a good deal of agricultural land for Israel. Flushed with victory, he returns home. And who should come out to meet him, celebrating his victory with singing and dancing, but his only child—a daughter.

Jephthah, of course, is horror-stricken. "Alas!" he cries, "I have triumphed over the enemy's army only to be defeated by a girl, my own daughter. Now it's impossible to erase the vow I took, since the Lord has already fulfilled his part. There's no escape from the terrible consequences of the promise I made."

Strangely enough, however, his daughter does not protest. In fact, she affirms that, the Lord having performed his part

107

of the bargain, her father has no choice but to carry through with his. She asks only one bit of leniency: that she be given a two-month reprieve. She will retreat to the mountains with her friends, mourning there for her virginity.

Now this strikes us as more than strange. It would seem that her first concern would be her own impending death, not her unused reproductive organs. Two cultural exigencies are operating here, however, that we need to be reminded of. First, the girl is powerless and knows it. Her father has, to her way of thinking, bartered her life for his military success. She could not withstand his resolve to carry through with the sacrifice, even if she tried. Second, at this point in their history, the only sort of afterlife the Hebrews understood was their genetic extension into the future. One was projected forward in time on the catapult of continuing generations. Once the genetic link was broken, one was left behind in the past while other members of the clan journeyed on in time. Dying a virgin, therefore, meant the end not just of one's present life but the loss of one's future life as well.

The story skips over the details of this woman's ritual death. We are left wondering just how this sacrifice was accomplished. Who actually plunged the knife into her heart or lit the funeral pyre? Human sacrifice played no part in the worship of Israel's God, and, in fact, was expressly forbidden. God is never reported to have endorsed the vow or demanded its fulfillment. Ever since he had tested Abraham's faith on Mount Moriah by demanding the sacrifice of Isaac, the prohibition of human sacrifice had been one of the distinguishing marks of the worship of Yahweh.

Interestingly, in his previous negotiations with the Ammonites Jephthah had mentioned the god Chemosh, to whom children were routinely sacrificed. "Be satisfied with the land Chemosh gives you," he says, "and we will possess what the Lord our God has given us." Obviously, Jephthah's religious understanding of his own deity is too limited and his recognition of Chemosh too substantial. Banished by his own people and thus cut off from authentic religious practice, Jephthah has grown muddled in his knowledge of Yahweh. His outlaw band has only a ragbag of cultic beliefs, brought with them from their various peoples. Desperate to prove himself to his old hometown, did he ignorantly fall back on a practice meant to honor Chemosh rather than Yahweh? He may have gotten the name right, but the content was all wrong. His religious confusion resulted in his daughter's death.

In an attempt to find something edifying about this story, commentators have often praised Jephthah's daughter for her obedience, for submitting to her father's misdirected piety. But the whole business was a sordid blot on Israel's history, in contrast to the story of Abraham and Isaac on Mount Moriah.

If there is any redeeming quality in this story it resides in Jephthah's resolve, but even more on his daughter's, to fulfill the vow that had been made. Keeping our word is not a virtue we're noted for today, and the fact that these two did gives them at least a modicum of tragic nobility. But the story of Jephthah's daughter stands as an illustration of Jesus' warning about binding vows made to the Lord. "Just say yes or no," he counseled. "Anything more than that can lead to trouble."

The story ends by explaining that ever afterward young Israelite girls customarily met for four days every year to lament Jephthah's daughter. Notice that they do not assemble in order to praise her for being a dutiful daughter, but to mourn her death. Lamentation is a far more fitting reaction to her story than praise.

Women and Violence

Enduring violence is one factor that marks the experience of women as distinctive from men's. While men are not immune to violence certainly, they are not systematically targeted as its object the way women are, both by virtue of their gender and their proportionately lesser strength.

Degrees of civilization can consistently be measured by the means cultures use both to circumscribe violence and to ensure justice based on something besides brute force. Law was one of humankind's greatest early gifts, providing some equity to human society. Though the law codes found in the Old Testament do not put men and women on an equal footing, they nevertheless went a long way toward providing legal protection to women of a sort they had not previously known. Punishments meted out for acts not even considered criminal today, such as adultery, were severe. Nevertheless, these laws were a step forward, since they implied women's responsibility as moral agents and prescribed equal punishment for men and women. One may question whether forcing a man to marry a woman he has raped would make for a happy home, but the impetus toward equitable reparation was nevertheless apparent in that law.

Many acts in the sexual realm, such as adultery, have been decriminalized today. Even rape, while still a crime, now receives a much less severe punishment. While it is also true that women enjoy greater freedom today, protection by the law has not increased. Women still suffer from violence just as brutal and live in just as much terror as women in the ancient world. And, like their ancient sisters, for no other reason than because they are women.

The stories in this section are not the ones you hear in Sunday school. Even those who think women are under-represented in the Bible cannot claim that their treatment has been whitewashed in these terrible tales. Appalling violence against women, particularly in the Old Testament, has been scrupulously chronicled.

The entire nineteenth chapter of Judges is devoted to an event so grisly it rivals even twentieth-century horror films. A woman, the concubine of a Levite priest, is gang-raped, murdered, and her body symbolically mutilated. Judges 19 is the only chapter in the Bible that ends with a direct cautionary note, as if the author himself were stunned into revulsion: "And it was so, that all that saw it said, There was no such deed done nor seen from the day that the children of Israel came up out of the land of Egypt unto this day: consider of it, take advice, and speak your minds."[1]

The last two chapters of Judges record the violent retribution for this act and its aftermath, an ending that only escalates the barbarity of the original crime. The book of Judges, in fact, closes with this line describing the social chaos that resulted from such crimes: "Every man did that which was right in his own eyes."[2]

Neither the mutilated concubine nor any of the other women who ultimately suffer for her vindication ever speak or take an active part in the story, however. We simply don't know, though we might imagine, what the events looked like from their point of view.

More enlightening are the accounts of Tamar, Rizpah, and the woman brought before Jesus to judge. In their stories we see not only the violent action but its effect on individual women.

TAMAR

2 Samuel 13:1-22; 1 Chronicles 3:9;
see also Exodus 22:16; Leviticus 18:9,7; 20:17;
Deuteronomy 22:28-29; 27:22

amar was the daughter of one king and the granddaughter of another, yet her position did not protect her from violence since it came from within the royal household itself. Tamar's mother was Maacah, daughter of the king of Geshur. David married Maacah during his rebel days in Hebron, possibly to secure his position among the Philistine warlords. She was not his first wife. Their first child, Absalom, was born there in Hebron, before David became king of Israel and moved his family to his new capital of Jerusalem.

Tamar, however, came along later when David had his full complement of eight wives, a number of concubines, and so many children he probably lost count. His only daughter and a city girl, Tamar never experienced those early years of hardship and war her older brothers had lived through; she had always lived in the palace. In the royal harem, in fact, along with the eight queens and their younger children. When we first see her, Tamar is still quite young. Even though neighboring rulers would see an alliance with a daughter of David's royal house as a political plum, she has not yet been married off.

The older boys, however, including Amnon and his half brother Absalom, are now grown men with their own houses. Amnon, David's eldest and the presumptive heir to the throne, falls in love with his young and beautiful half-sister Tamar. His unfulfilled desire becomes such an obsession that he begins to waste away. Observing this, his cousin Jonadab, a nephew of David and "very subtil,"[1] induces Amnon to confess his love for Tamar—whom he calls "my brother Absalom's sister,"[2] downplaying his own kinship to her.

Jonadab, who may have had his own political reasons for stirring up trouble in his uncle's royal household, suggests a plan. "Go to bed," he tells Amnon, "and pretend you're sick. When your father comes to check on you, tell him the only thing you can even think about eating are those heart-shaped dumplings Tamar makes. Say you can eat them only if she comes and makes them right here in your sight." This latter stipulation would lead David to believe that Amnon suspects he is being poisoned by someone in his household and will only trust food that his own sister makes.

The plan works. David comes to visit his sick son, hears his request, and immediately sends back to the palace for Tamar to come fix the special dumplings for her brother. Amnon's desire kindles as he watches the girl mixing and kneading the dough, then baking the heart-shaped dumplings. When they are done, she brings them to him.

He, however, still refuses to eat. "Everyone out," he commands, "except for Tamar." When the servants and bodyguards are gone, he tells his sister, "Now, bring the dumplings in here to my bedroom. I want you to feed me yourself." And again, of course, she complies.

She approaches, holding out the dish to him, but Amnon grabs her arm. "Forget the dumplings," he says, "it's you I want."

Terrified, Tamar pulls back, appealing to his moral sense

and Israel's law against incest. "No, brother, please don't humiliate me in this way. We don't do this kind of thing. Not in Israel. It's unspeakable, unthinkable. Please! Don't!"

But Amnon drags her down.

"Please don't!" she begs. "Where will I go? What will happen to me? And to you, Amnon," she adds in her desperation, appealing now to his political ambition. "This will wreck your chances of being king. People will think you're crazy."

But Amnon is unrelenting.

Desperate now, Tamar grasps at straws, invoking the Mosaic Law that requires a man who seduces a virgin to marry her. "Not like this. Just ask our father. Then he'll give me to you, I know he will."

But Amnon is in no mood to wait.

Hebrew has no noun for rape. When Tamar said it was "unspeakable" she meant it literally; she calls rape "the thing that ought not to be done." There is no verb for rape in Hebrew either. It employs the same term it uses to describe the enslavement of the Israelites by the Egyptians—"to humble."

After raping, and thus humbling, his sister, Amnon suddenly feels nothing but loathing for her. No longer is she his fresh young sister, captivating with her blooming beauty. In his sight she is now only a piece of defiled flesh. The text emphasizes his reaction: his hate for her was greater than the desire that had formerly consumed him. "Get up and get out of my sight," he snarls.

"What am I supposed to do now?" she wails. "You've ruined me."

But Amnon only wants to be rid of her. He calls his personal servant and tells him to throw her out. "And lock the door after her!" he cries. Obediently, the servant shows her to the door and locks it against her.

Tamar stands abandoned in the street outside. Her long-sleeved robe marks her for all the world to see as the king's unmarried daughter. A princess. For all the good that has done her. Her royal position has not protected her against the lust and power of her own brother. She stoops down and scoops up a handful of dust and throws it on her head, the symbol of her degradation. She grasps her princess robe in both hands and rips it open, a sign of her mourning. Then she wanders off down the streets of Jerusalem, moaning and sobbing, until she stumbles into someone—her brother Absalom.

After listening to her story, he takes her back to his house. Yet the counsel he offers her is hardly consoling. "Hush," he tells her. "After all, he is your brother. Don't make a big deal out of it. Just forget it." He seems unaware that her rapist's kinship makes the violation even worse. And neither Tamar nor God can put it aside and forget about incest and rape.

Tamar's future is ruined. She is cut off from the possibilities of marriage or children. Henceforth she will live in her brother Absalom's house, while the evil consequences of Amnon's act play themselves out.

Word of the incestuous rape comes to the king her father. And though it angers him, he nevertheless takes no action. He doesn't insist on bringing Tamar back to the palace. Certainly he does not move to punish his firstborn son.

Meanwhile, brother Absalom bides his time. For two years he keeps his peace, staying away from his older brother to avoid a confrontation. Then one spring he invites all of his brothers out to his place in the country to celebrate the end of sheepshearing season, a traditional time of festivity. Once Amnon has had enough to drink to let down his guard, Absalom tells his servants they are to fall upon his brother and assassinate the brute.

Absalom has already made plans to escape after his brother's murder and seek refuge with his maternal grandfather, the king of Geshur. For the next three years he hides out there, plotting a revolt against his father, one that will end in his own death and inflict on his father David the worst loss he ever sustains, one from which he never fully recovers.

We hear no more of Tamar. But the placement of her sad story in the saga of Israel's greatest king is instructive.

It follows immediately the story of David's own adultery with Bathsheba and his engineering of her husband's death so he could have her for his own. Amnon, then, had only been following in his father's footsteps when he decides to flout the law against incest that would deny him the woman he wants. His father, he must have figured, got away with it. Why shouldn't he? Perhaps then, David's failure to enforce the law against his son was owing to his own sense of past guilt.

True, David did not rape Bathsheba. But did she come willingly when the king sent his henchmen to fetch her? Would there have been any point in protesting? We don't know.

Tamar, however, did protest, using every argument available to her. She appealed to any innate moral sense Amnon might have had, to Israel's laws against incest and against rape, to reason, and finally to her brother's pride and political ambition. Nothing worked. And afterward, instead of crawling off, trying to conceal the crime against her, she publicly announced it in the streets of Jerusalem. If she couldn't protect herself, she could at least expose the crime, even though it meant her own shame.

The story of Tamar's rape is all too psychologically and socially accurate. Rape is such a primitive crime that its essential elements haven't changed in the last three thousand years. Sexual obsession consumes both the person who harbors it and the person who is its object. Like the will to power, it is immune to reason. Once the obsession is sated, the void it leaves inevitably fills with loathing. And a society that, like David's, tolerates it, offering its victims not justice but only concealment, becomes impotent against the consequences of that evil.

RIZPAH
2 Samuel 3:6-11, 21:1-14

*M*aybe she was a raving beauty whose good looks were the catalyst for a disaster. Maybe she was simply being used as a pawn in a power play by an ambitious military man. Whatever the unrecorded particulars of the case, Rizpah's private tragedy is buried at the heart of a larger tale of intrigue and political maneuvering—and not without purpose.

After Israel's first king, Saul, and his son Jonathan were killed in battle, the country passed into the hands of Saul's second and much weaker son, Ish-Bosheth. The real power behind the throne, however, was Abner, the general who had led Saul's army. Whether as a means of solidifying his position as quasi king or because he had hankered after Saul's concubine for some time, no sooner was the old king dead than Abner claimed Rizpah for himself. Ish-Bosheth objected to the general taking such liberties with his dead father's concubine. It showed flagrant disrespect for Saul's memory, he said. (If anyone consulted Rizpah herself on the matter, it is not recorded.)

Abner exploded. "You have me to thank for saving you from David's army. And all you can do is criticize me for taking what should have been given to me as a reward!" Ish-Bosheth, quaking in his royal sandals, was too intimidated by the general to respond.

This further demonstration of his king's weakness must have pushed Abner over the edge. At any rate, he seized the occasion to change sides in Israel's six-year struggle with David's rebel forces. After conferring in secret with the elders of Israel, he set out with a delegation to Hebron, David's stronghold, and cut a deal with him. Abner hadn't reckoned, however, with the jealousy of David's own general, Joab. Before Abner could return to Jerusalem, Joab lured him into an ambush and murdered him.

How did this conspiracy affect Rizpah's fortunes back in Jerusalem? We're not told. With Abner dead, she would have little protection during the siege of the city that followed. Ish-Bosheth cannot shield her since he himself is killed by a couple of his own mercenaries, who decide to throw in their lot with David. However, since David, ever faithful to his old master Saul, has Ish-Bosheth's murderers hung and their mutilated bodies publicly displayed as a warning to those who would harm any of Saul's offspring, it's possible that Rizpah's connection to Saul ensured her protection and maintenance.

At any rate, she is still around several years later when David, now firmly established in the unified kingdom, has to deal with a three-year famine brought on by drought. When he inquires of the Lord as to the famine's cause, he is told that Saul left behind a piece of unfinished business. It seems that at some point in his reign, during the height of his military exploits, Saul promised to spare a group called the Gibeonites from slaughter. Obviously, Saul must have reneged on his promise—though the details of this battle are not recorded in the Bible—because now the Gibeonites are seeking restitution, and the Lord is taking their side by withholding rain from Israel until the matter is cleared up. David offers to make a cash settlement, but the Gibeonites refuse to accept anything but the hardest of currencies—blood. The blood of Saul's heirs. Seven of them.

David himself is now caught between vows. Having promised Jonathan that he would look after his children, David cannot hand over his friend's son Mephibosheth to the Gibeonites. So he gives them instead the five sons of Saul's daughter Merab. Plus Saul's only surviving sons, the children of the concubine Rizpah.

One fine spring morning, the seven are impaled by the Gibeonites on a mountaintop near Saul's hometown. The bodies are to be left there, exposed all summer long till the time when the autumn rains should begin, which will signal the end of the drought and famine.

Now, for the first time, Rizpah enters the story as something more than a sexual pawn in political maneuvering. She takes action—the only action possible for a woman in her shaky position. Certainly neither she nor Merab could protect their sons from death. But after enduring that inevitability, Rizpah still performs the only meaningful deed open to her. Carrying sackcloth up to the mountain where the sacrificial victims have been left exposed to the elements, she spreads it over the bodies. Then she camps out there all summer long. During the day she beats off the vultures that would otherwise peck out the eyes and entrails of the corpses. At night she fends off the jackals that would strip the flesh from the skeletons and scatter the bones.

At this point, Rizpah's macabre vigil reminds me of Antigone's from Greek tragedy. In Sophocles' play, the daughter of the deposed king Oedipus opposes her uncle Creon by symbolically honoring the corpse of her slain brother who had been left to lie exposed to the sun and vultures as a warning to other rebels. And certainly both of these stories show how ancient cultures set great store on honoring the dead by not allowing desecration of the body. Antigone's defiance earned her own death and her country more suffering, while Rizpah's humble efforts proved to be the hinge that turned events toward renewed health for the land.

Word of how Rizpah is defending the dead bodies from desecration eventually makes its way to David's ear. No doubt feeling reproached by her pitiful devotion, the king follows her example. He has the bones of Saul and Jonathan retrieved from Jabesh-gilead and buried in the family sepulcher—along with the sacrificed remains of Saul's sons and grandsons.

And interestingly, it is *then*, rather than after the sacrificial slaughter of Saul's progeny, that God answers the prayers for an end to the famine. Was it mercy he desired all along, and not sacrifice? Go back and read the story closely and you'll see that, when David finally consulted the Lord after three years of famine, he was told merely that the present hard times were the result of Saul and his blood-crazed heirs killing the Gibeonites off in a frenzy of "ethnic cleansing." He was given no instructions as to how to amend the situation. Never did the Lord order David to accede to the Gibeonites' wishes for human sacrifice. Nor, for that matter, did David ask.

It was only later, after David heard of Rizpah's pitifully desperate measures, that it occurred to him to follow suit and give his old enemy Saul and his heirs a "decent burial." And because of that long-delayed display of mercy, the land was healed.

Rizpah's story also reminds me of a contemporary woman, Yvonne Bezejah, a Brazilian socialite, whose life of privilege was dramatically challenged one night when she witnessed the slaughter of six "street kids" in the Candeleria district of Rio de Janeiro. The city's thieves often recruit abandoned children to steal for them, creating a crime problem for the Rio police. On that night alone, the extermination squad had rounded up and killed sixty children in different parts of the city. Across the street from Rio's largest church, Yvonne stood watch all night over the bodies of six children to keep the police from disposing of the bodies. A lone woman, she could not stop the slaughter, but her vigil exposed to the world the hideous truth beneath Rio's veneer of wealth and glamor.

Looking back from our vantage point of three millennia, it is easy to find plenty to object to in Rizpah's story. The practice of concubinage itself. Abner's demonstrating his power by claiming rights to her sexual use. Her sons publicly butchered. But we are all circumscribed in one way or another by the age in which we live. Cultural strictures often keep us from both seeing and acting upon opportunities to show mercy. We do more honor to Rizpah and her womanhood by focusing instead on how she made the most of her one small opportunity. She wasn't given a lot of latitude, either by her culture or her circumstances. After everything had been taken away from her—her youth, her beauty, her male protectors—she took what she still had—her mother's grief—and acted upon it. And taught a lesson to Israel's greatest king that saved his nation.

WOMAN TAKEN IN ADULTERY

John 8:1-11

hough an authentic story about Jesus, this narrative became detached at some point from its original setting—in Luke, most biblical scholars agree—since it shares much both in style and content with that gospel. The story eventually found its way into the Gospel of John where it seems to fit remarkably well. For one thing, the previous chapter of John records a number of controversies between Jesus and the Pharisees over issues of law and judgment, which is the theme of this story. At least twice in that chapter Jesus' enemies have wanted to arrest him but hold back, succumbing to a strange hesitancy to lay hands on him.

Thus the way is prepared for this account of a woman whom no one shrinks from seizing or judging. She has, after all, been caught in the act—in bed with someone else's husband. Or maybe she was someone else's wife. Maybe both of them were married. Whatever the circumstances, it's a clearcut case of adultery, and she is dragged from bed, probably naked, through the streets, and shoved in front of Jesus.

The hands that have seized her are those of his enemies—the same scribes and Pharisees who so far have been afraid to grab him and carry him off to prison. Jesus would not fail to realize that this woman is taking the brunt of their anger and indignation because they're reluctant to direct it toward him. Up until now the conflict between Jesus and the religious establishment has been confined to verbal battles. But with this act of seizing the woman the violence has become physical.

"Rabbi," they say (and he would hear the derision in their tone), "we caught her in bed with this guy—in the very act. You know what the Mosaic Law says about this." Only the day before, Jesus had been lecturing them about Moses and the Law, saying that none of them kept it. *Don't judge by appearances,* he'd said. Fine. Here was more than just appearances. This woman stood before him now in living color, her sin undeniable. Let him try to wiggle out of this. He'd have to come down foursquare for law and order now or lose his credibility with the people.

"We ought to stone her, right? That's what the law says," they insist.

Actually, however, the law in Deuteronomy states that stoning is a punishment for women who are unfaithful to men they are betrothed to. Also, in the case of adultery, both participants are to be executed, and the method is not prescribed. Thus Jesus could in fact have debated these finer points of the law with them. However, Jesus knows it's not adultery they're worried about. They're simply seeking a pretext to discredit him with the people.

"You go along with the law, don't you?" they continue to prod. The very question implies, of course, that they suspect—even hope—that he won't.

He sits there silently for a moment. They've encircled him like predators holding their quarry at bay, moving in for the kill. Then Jesus does something he does nowhere else in the Bible. He bends over and writes with his finger on the ground. No doubt they expected him to leap to his feet in order to counter their own threatening stance, to wave his arms in a gesture of opposition and defiance. Instead, he stoops even lower. This unlooked-for reaction, along with his pre-occupied doodling, takes them entirely off guard.

"Hey, didn't you hear?" What *is* he doing anyway?

Once they're in a state of true perplexity rather than merely feigning uncertainty over his opinion, Jesus rises. The initial explosiveness of the situation has by now been defused, and his answer can be felt as authority rather than as bickering.

"All right," he says, startling them. Then he adds, "If you're certain of your own innocence, then go ahead." And, bending down once more, he begins to write again.

Who knows what he was writing. All speculations remain just that—guesses. Perhaps it was another passage from Deuteronomy, one they've obviously forgotten: *You must be blameless before the Lord your God.*[1] Or the stipulation, also from Deuteronomy, that requires the first hand raised to execute a condemned person be that of the accuser.[2]

Who wouldn't hesitate at that moment? After all, these are not barbarians Jesus is talking to, not thugs or hooligans who in fact get a kick out of violence for its own sake. They are respectable people, the educated elite. They believe in capital punishment for adultery—on principle. But not if theirs is the hand that has to do the dirty work.

What makes them hesitate now to pick up those stones to hurl at the woman but their very education, their knowledge of the law they are trying to use against Jesus. Knowing that they have not in fact followed the letter of the law, which requires them to bring the male offender also, each of them also knowing some secret infraction he has committed against the law, no one can bring himself to bend over and pick up the first rock. Jesus does not look up from his writing, does not challenge them with even a glance. Finally, the eldest man, who remembers most, turns and leaves. He is followed by another and another, until at last all the accusers have disappeared.

During this scene, attention has been diverted from the woman herself. Jesus waits till all the men are gone before he looks up again. The woman is still standing there before him. The moment for truth has come.

"Where has everyone gone?" he asks her. "Have they all dropped their charges? Isn't anyone left to accuse you?"

And the woman herself finally speaks, for the first and only time. Not to defend herself, but simply to answer his question. "No one, Lord."[3]

"All right," he says. "Then I won't be the one to punish you either. Now you're free to go. But don't do it again."

Thus he releases her while at the same time asserting his right to judge her. Jesus is the blameless one, the only one whose hand could justifiably be raised against her. He has waited until they were alone to tell her this, however. He is her judge, indeed, her only judge.

What is clear from this story is that, without Jesus' intervention, this woman would have borne the consequences of this crime both for herself and her equally guilty partner. It's no good looking around for him in the crowd. He's obviously slunk off to hide somewhere. No knight in shining armor, he hasn't tried to protect her from the mob that stormed in and dragged her out of the house nor has he followed to make any protest on her behalf. Pitiful in his cowardice, he's been entirely willing to let her take the blame for them both.

Jesus, on the other hand, has calmed the violence of this storm as effectually as he did the storm on the lake. He has not backed down in the face of the threatening crowd but has provided the woman protection in a way more miraculous than if he had turned all her accusers to toads—by prompting them to examine their own consciences.

Tamar and Jephthah's daughter were innocent victims of violence. This woman, however, is not innocent. Though we may find the punishment for adultery excessive, we have to admit that the *cost* of adultery, not just in terms of damaged emotions but measured in actual effects on human lives, is enormous. Like all crime, it is destructive. Who pays for that devastation and waste? The moral universe, like the physical one, is a delicately balanced equation. Its deficits have to be made up somehow.

The violence that would have been wreaked on this guilty woman will now be directed toward Jesus. By refusing to punish her, he has gathered her guilt to himself. The sin is no less sin for having the sentence commuted; it will still have consequences. But he is the one who will bear them—and in only a few more days—in her place.

Sensual Women

Two basic dangers plague the human race. We are both physical and spiritual beings, yet we find it almost impossible to balance those two supposedly contradictory aspects of our nature. Some of us, preferring the pure ideal to messy reality, are tempted to live in a realm of ethereal abstraction where bodies are only a nuisance and encumbrance. Others, impatient with what they can't see or touch, insist that the senses are the only reality and their gratification life's sole reward.

Dealing with the senses is particularly perplexing for contemporary women. For one thing, our culture assumes we are made of nothing but nerve endings constantly screaming to be stimulated. Ads for clothes, jewelry, perfume, and makeup pay the freight in women's magazines. Articles in those publications routinely feature food, sex, and something called "beauty" as their primary stock-in-trade. Unfortunately, the women's movement has done surprisingly little to change these assumptions.

Sensory perception is essential to being human. We ignore that at our peril. Even more, our senses are the good gift of God. He put the first man and woman in a garden where he planted "every tree that is pleasant to the sight, and good for food,"[1] specifically to gratify their senses. The name of the place is most accurately translated "Garden of Delight." Realizing that these creatures required more than spiritual communion, he provided them flesh-and-blood comfort through each other's body.

Yet it is also through the senses that Eve is tempted. The

fruit of the forbidden tree that she eats to make her wise first attracts her because "it was pleasant to the eyes."[2] And ever afterwards, women have found it difficult to achieve that lost balance between wisdom and feeling. They have been caught in the web of desire, often reduced to objects of appetite themselves. When love becomes lust, the garden becomes a jungle.

The stories here provide a spectrum of sensual women— women who, far from denying their senses, engage them in very different ways. On one end is Potiphar's wife, a sexual predator, who operates by the law of the jungle. Midway, the song of the Shulammite maiden shows the pathos of an attempt to recapture love in the garden, one doomed to fail because her beauty makes her a prize trophy. Yet on the far end of the spectrum, the difficult balance is attained in one epiphanic moment when Mary of Bethany manifests her ideal love within the world of the senses.

POTIPHAR'S WIFE

Genesis 39

We don't know much about Potiphar's wife, not even her name. She plays, after all, only a bit part in the story of Joseph. We can infer, however, that she was not a happy woman, despite the fact that her husband was a high-ranking military man, a captain of Pharaoh's guard, with entreé to the Egyptian court.

This detail proves important in the unfolding story of Joseph, Jacob's best-beloved son whose spiteful brothers have sold the seventeen-year-old boy as a slave to traders traveling down to Egypt. Though one disaster after another plagues Joseph, he appears to lead a charmed life. After every setback he bounces back to an even higher position.

When the traders sell him in Egypt, it is Potiphar, the captain of the guard, who buys this handsome specimen of young manhood. Potiphar puts him in charge of his household and eventually makes him manager of all his property. So well does Joseph handle his master's affairs that soon Potiphar turns over all decisions to this servant with the golden touch. After a while, except for what is set before him on the table, Potiphar no longer even knows how much he owns or what it is worth.

His wife, however, has other hungers.

Joseph would find Egyptian women quite different from the ones he remembers at home. For one thing, they live in houses rather than wandering from place to place with their large extended families, camping in tents, and constantly searching for water and grass for their herds, as the women in his family do.

Potiphar's wife, however, seems unable to appreciate the advantages of her more settled life. She roams from room to room, restless, dissatisfied. With him managing every household detail, there's little for her to do indoors all day. But shouldn't that make her life easier? His own poor mother, who had died when he was still a small boy, certainly never knew the luxury of lounging about on a sofa, sighing with boredom and discontent. She never even had a sofa. For that matter, Joseph himself had never seen any proper furniture until he came to Egypt.

Nor had he seen women paint their faces before he came to this strange land. His master's wife lines her already dark eyes in black kohl and rubs finely powdered red clay on her cheeks. The clothes she wears are made of linen so delicately woven you can see right through it, unlike the sturdy wool his sisters' tunics and cloaks are made of. These Egyptian women believe in showing as much as possible, instead of covering themselves up. They'd never dream of covering their heads. Since they spend most of their time indoors, they don't bother to protect themselves from the sun in the way of nomads but go about with bare arms and shoulders.

No doubt a young man like Joseph finds the very strangeness of Egyptian women titillating. And Potiphar's wife, though probably older than he, would certainly be a temptation. However, Joseph knows enough to be cautious. He has some experience of cunning women who plot and maneuver to get what they want. It's a family legend, the way his grandmother

Rebekah schemed to have the paternal blessing fall on his own father Jacob's head instead of his uncouth uncle Esau's. And when their family's caravan left the far north country of Padan-Aram for Canaan, his own mother had outsmarted her father by stealing his household gods to pay back the wily old man for all the misery he caused her.

So Joseph is on his guard when his master's wife begins to cast sidelong glances his way. Strangers and their ways have always been a threat to his nomadic people. Though he was just a child at the time, he remembers when his half-sister Dinah had tried to pay a friendly visit to girlfriends in Shechem and been raped. And he remembers the terrible consequences that followed too—how his brothers concocted a barbaric plot in revenge, one that ended with the family having to leave the green valley and move on once more. It was that trek that had finally caused his mother, pregnant with the only other child she bore in that sprawling, brawling family, to go into labor and die in childbirth. All because his sister Dinah had been too friendly with strangers.

No, he thinks, *I've only survived in Egypt because I've watched my p's and q's. No one with my background can afford to let down his guard around these city folk.*

So when his master's wife resorts to more obvious ploys to get Joseph's attention, he's prepared. One day she calls him into the shadowy interior of her quarters and actually propositions him.

Joseph backs away nervously.

"Come on," she says, puckering her mouth into a pout, "No one will know."

Right, Joseph thinks. *I'm the outsider, the stranger here, and you say I won't be tossed to the crocodiles if we're discovered in bed together? Sure, lady.* The only way out of this potentially dangerous situation, he believes, is to remind her of the trust his master has put in him.

"Your poor husband," he says, "think of him. Potiphar doesn't even know what goes on in his own house," he says.

"He trusts me with everything. He's put me in charge of his entire household. The only thing he hasn't given me is you. What kind of gratitude would I be showing if I were to repay his generosity by stealing his wife? It would be a crime against him and God." And he backs cautiously out of the room.

The lady, however, is not discouraged. Maybe she finds his reticence charming. Maybe it stimulates her passion to see him confused and blushing. At any rate, she's undeterred. Determined to have him, her advances become ever more flagrant. She's not a woman used to being denied, especially by some young twit who, after all, is only a slave. Besides, his boast about being master of the house hasn't gone down well. Her desire takes on the harder edge of demand.

But Joseph, determined to avoid her advances, finds plenty to do outdoors in the field where he feels safer. Possibly he even arranges to sleep in the barn and eat his meals in the open air. He cannot, however, evade his duties indoors altogether. The accounts, for instance, must be kept up.

So one day he slips indoors to go over the books. All is quiet within the house. Everyone seems to have vanished. Nervous at the silence and the absence of the other servants, he goes about his business and is just creeping out again when he hears her calling to him from her bedroom. Caught!

He goes and stands in the doorway.

"Come closer, Joseph," she murmurs. "I've missed you."

He takes a step toward her.

She pats the bed beside her. "Everyone's gone. You don't have to worry. Now's our chance. No one will ever know." She holds out her hand to him.

He's petrified. She frowns at his lack of response.

"No, ma'am, I can't."

Her frown deepens. If the little country bumpkin doesn't know any better than to pass up an invitation like this—

But Joseph is already backing away. She can't believe it. What if he tells Potiphar? This foreign upstart already has her husband wrapped around his little finger. What if Potiphar believes him? Quick as a striking viper she grabs Joseph's tunic.

He tries to pull loose but she gives a vicious tug, perhaps thinking his nakedness will force him to stay. But he runs from the room, stripped, her mocking laughter following him as he flees. The servants he encounters in the courtyard stare at him as he runs past. Then the laughter turns to loud shrieks. "Help!" she's shouting. "Help me. I've been attacked."

The other servants hurry in and find the woman sprawled beside her disheveled bed, clutching Joseph's tunic. "Look," she says, "look what the barbarian tried to do to me. He tried to rape me right in my own house. No wonder he thinks he can get away with anything. You've heard him brag about being master of the house. He thought he could have me along with everything else."

The servants look uneasily at one another. It cannot have escaped their notice that their mistress has been eyeing the young Hebrew slave. On the other hand, if Joseph treated them as he had his brothers, lording it over them, the Egyptian servants would have no more love for him than his brothers did. And after all, he *is* a foreigner, one of those alien workers who never settle down. No telling what they might try.

When Potiphar comes home that evening, his wife is waiting for him. Still clutching Joseph's torn tunic, she goes through her story again, emphasizing her husband's bad judgment in bringing a stranger into the house and giving him too much power. "You set him up here as lord and master in your place. No wonder it's gone to his head." Stressing also Joseph's foreignness. "You know nothing at all about this kid," she sobs. "For all you know he could be an axe-murderer. You should have heard him mock me when I wouldn't submit to him."

Needless to say, this is the end of Joseph's upward mobility—at least for a while. Off he goes to prison. Though considering that the penalty could well have been death, we have to wonder if Potiphar wasn't a little suspicious of his wife's tale.

As for her, however, history has meted out a punishment that fits her crime exactly. Potiphar's wife became a stock figure used to admonish readers in countless Jewish and Christian scriptural commentaries. She appears in the Islamic Koran as well where she is given a name—"Suleika." She turns up in Persian epos, Spanish drama, and Middle English poems. In *Pilgrim's Progress*, Bunyan makes her the allegorical figure Wanton. Perhaps cruelest of all is Henry Fielding's portrait in his novel *Joseph Andrews*, where she appears as Lady Booby, an aging beauty who tries to seduce her young servant.

It is, in fact, the very desperation of the woman's desire that makes her either a comic or pitiful figure, depending on one's sensibilities. Our culture tends to romanticize sensuality, making it almost a religion in itself. People torn by passion are seen to be in the grip of some divine, ecstatic madness. But only when they are young and beautiful. We tend to ridicule the sexual hunger of older women for younger men.

However, the most chilling aspect of this story of Potiphar's wife is how quickly the heat of her passion hardened into hatred. Not love, but malice was the fruit of her disappointed sensuality.

SHULAMMITE MAIDEN

The Song of Songs

*B*ecause of its erotic content and the fact that it does not mention God's name, the biblical book titled "The Song of Songs" or "The Song of Solomon" barely made it into the Hebrew Bible. Rabbis disagreed about including it among the scrolls to be read on special occasions up until the first century AD when a rabbinical council finalized the contents of Jewish scripture. But its supporters were adamant. In its defense, Rabbi Akiba wrote: "The whole age altogether is not equal to the day on which the Song of Songs was given to Israel."

Reconstructing the book's story line is an arduous task. For one thing, it is not a prose narrative but a cycle of lyric poems spoken by three characters—a shepherd, his lover, and Solomon, the king. At times a group known as "daughters of Jerusalem" also speak, much as the chorus does in ancient Greek drama. But figuring out the story from these dialogue poems is much like reconstituting the plot of a musical or an opera when all you have are the songs or arias.

Nevertheless, the Song of Songs is the closest approximation to drama the Bible supplies, since Semitic cultures were not familiar with theater. But the author furnishes no stage directions and does not even identify the speakers of the various parts. Thus, it's often difficult to decipher references or even tell what speech belongs to which character. In fact, because of these problems the book has been divided into as many as thirty-one or as few as fourteen separate poems.

Since a large portion of the book comes to us in the voice of the Shulammite maiden, without the mediation of a male narrator, we come as close to hearing a woman's true voice speaking from the ancient world in the Song of Songs as anywhere else in Scripture. Because of this, some scholars have even speculated that the author was herself a woman.

This is the way I reconstruct the plot of the story. A pretty country girl catches the eye of the king and is brought to Jerusalem as an addition to King Solomon's extensive harem (seven hundred women seems to be the round figure for its population). Possibly she comes from Shunem or Sulam overlooking the Valley of Jezreel, not far from the Plain of Esdralon, though the poems contain place names from as far north as Syria to as far south as the Negev desert.

At any rate, it is clear that she is a country girl. Though she is "comely,"[1] she compares her dark skin to the black tents of Kedar. She tells the "daughters of Jerusalem,"[2] possibly the other members of the harem, that she is so dark because her brothers have forced her to work out in the hot sun in the family's vineyards in order to punish her. Why are they angry with their little sister? We don't know. She only hints metaphorically with the line "mine own vineyard have I not kept."[3]

We can assume though that the brothers' anger has something to do with her next question: where is her lover pasturing his flocks? The lover responds by telling her to follow the sheep trail till she comes to the shepherds' tents. Evidently, she finds him there, because a love-duet follows. While the king sits at his table in the city, the Shulammite and her shepherd relish one another on their bed of green under cedar and fir branches that form the living beams and rafters of their roof.

In the second chapter, the delicate intimacies between the two lovers are described in sensory images of nature. Apple trees, grapevines, fig trees, the rose of Sharon, lily of the valley—figures of delight and fruitfulness portray both their bodies and their love. When the shepherd comes to call her out to the countryside, he leaps and skips down the mountain like a young deer, then stands at her window calling through the lattice, "Rise up, my love, my fair one, and come away. For, lo, the winter is past, the rain is over and gone; the flowers appear on the earth; the time of the singing of birds is come, and the voice of the turtle[dove] is heard in our land; the fig tree putteth forth her green figs, and the vines with the tender grape give a good smell. Arise, my love, my fair one, and come away."[4]

The scene changes in chapter three, however, to the city where the girl is now cut off from her lover. She searches through the streets for him, even boldly approaching the city watchmen to ask if they have seen him. Eventually she finds him, but their reunion is short-lived.

The imagery changes abruptly, signaling a change in both the tone of the poem and the fortunes of the young woman. She is the property of the king now, and sixty of his warriors are dispatched to fetch her back to the palace, their chariots raising a pillar of dust in the wilderness. Led to Solomon's bed, she finds it luxuriant, made not of field grass and tree branches, but crafted with silver and gold and covered with purple, the color of royalty. However, it is also surrounded by warriors; swords hang on their thighs "because of fear in the night."[5]

Whether she is seduced by the king's wealth and splendor or whether she knows resistance is futile, chapter 4 shows the king making love to the Shulammite. Though his extravagant praise of her beauty begins by using pastoral metaphors, comparing her hair to a flock of goats on Mount Gilead and her teeth to "sheep that are even shorn,"[6] the wild, natural imagery the king uses to describe her beauty gradually modulates to tamer, more domesticated analogies. She becomes an enclosed park, a dammed-up spring, a sealed fountain. Such, we feel, is the consequence of belonging to the king. The liberty and freedom she's known before is traded for the opulent confinement of the harem.

She signals her capitulation to the king and her captivity within the garden walls in the last verse of the fourth chapter: "Awake, O north wind; and come, thou south; blow upon my garden, that the spices thereof may flow out. Let my beloved come into his garden, and eat his pleasant fruits."[7] She is now Solomon's garden, and her fruits are his for the taking. He answers her: "I am come into my garden, my sister, my spouse: I have gathered my myrrh with my spice; I have eaten my honeycomb with my honey."[8]

In the meantime, however, the shepherd has not forgotten her. He comes to the city to find her, his head still wet with dew. "Open to me, my sister, my love," he pleads. He even calls her "my undefiled," letting her know with admirable delicacy that her yielding to the king has not lowered her in his eyes.[9]

She contradicts his generous assessment of her situation, however, answering him metaphorically: "I have put off my coat; how shall I put it on?" Then, perhaps to tease him, perhaps to test him, she plays on the word *defile* by giving it another meaning: "I have washed my feet; how shall I defile them?"[10] No longer a country girl, she is now a member of the royal harem, bathed, perfumed, a pampered city lady. Yet when she sees his hand at the latch, she cannot resist him and rises to let the shepherd in.

But when she opens the door, he has already fled. She calls after him, but there is no answer.

She slips out to search for him. But this time when the city watchmen find her out of the harem confines, they are not so gentle. They strip her veil away, beat her, and drag her back to the palace. She pleads with the other women in the harem to find her beloved and tell him she is lovesick for him.

They answer her with mocking cynicism, "Tell us, O Fairest-Among-Women, how is one man any better than another? Isn't one lover much the same as another? Why should *we* look for him?"

She answers them with seven verses extolling the beauty of her shepherd, ending with "This is my beloved, and this is my friend,"[11] the only time the word *friend* is used between a man and woman in the Old Testament. Does this also signal a shift in her perception of their relationship?

At any rate, the harem women, her words perhaps having roused their own memories of freely given love, are moved to help her search for the shepherd. When they find him, however, his praise for the Shulammite has undergone a subtle change. In addition to the earlier natural imagery, he ranks her as superlative to the king's other women—the sixty queens, eighty concubines, and virgins without number. He places her present royal status beyond his own reach: "Who is this that suddenly appears like the dawn, fair as the moon, shining like the sun, a procession of heavenly bodies? I only came down to check on my orchard and see if the vines have budded or if the pomegranates were in bloom, but before I knew what was happening, I found myself surrounded by chariots from the king's household."

The harem women, recognizing the distance that now separates the two lovers, call to the Shulammite to return to the palace. They see the two forces contending for her— the shepherd's love and the king's—and already know which will win.

The first part of the seventh chapter is the farewell song of the shepherd to the Shulammite. Though he mixes echoes of earlier nature imagery to describe her, he accents again her current regal status. She's no longer a barefoot lass who can leap about the mountainside with him. Instead, "How beautiful are thy feet with shoes, O prince's daughter," he sings, "the joints of thy thighs are like jewels, the work of the hands of a cunning workman."[12] He acknowledges that she now belongs to the king: "Thine head upon thee is like Carmel, and the hair of thine head like purple; the king is held in the galleries."[13]

"But I am yours," she protests. "Come, we'll go out to the fields again. We'll get up early and go to the vineyards to see if the vines are flourishing, whether there are any grapes or pomegranates yet. There we will make love like before. I've been saving up my love to give to you."

But the impossibility of their love is beginning to dawn on her too. "If only you were my brother," she says, "then when I saw you outside the harem I could kiss you without fear of reprisal. I could take you home with me to my mother's house where we could delight ourselves in safety." The conditional nature of this song shows she comprehends the futility of their love.

Using the "envelope structure" of Hebrew poetry, many verses in this last chapter echo the first part of the book. For example, in the book's first poem she described their love like this: "His left hand is under my head, and his right hand doth embrace me." Now she subtly changes the words to "His left hand *should be* under my head and his right hand *should embrace* me."[14] She ends her own farewell song to the shepherd by repeating another verse from that first song, though once more she makes a slight change that reflects her altered fortunes: "I charge you, O ye daughters of Jerusalem," she had said earlier when she felt their love was invulnerable, "by the roes, and by the hinds of the field, that ye stir not up, nor awake my love, till he please."[15] Now she eliminates the references to roes and hinds of the field. After all, that life of freedom is behind her now. And she changes the charge to a plaintive question: "Why should you stir up, or why awake my love, until he please?"[16]

Then she leaves the wilderness behind forever. She returns to the city, the harem women note, not leaping but leaning upon the arm of her beloved. Her last words to the shepherd are a testimony to her enduring love for him but also a warning that the king's jealousy is a fire that can consume them both. The only consolation she can offer is that, despite the king's power, his riches cannot buy her love.

In the second half of chapter eight the new princess reflects ironically on how her brothers schemed to profit from her when she was still just a child. "If she turns out to be a wall," they said, "we will build upon her a palace of silver: but if she's only a door, we'll shut her up with boards of cedar." Well, she thinks now, I turned out to be a wall—my breasts were like towers—so the king wanted me. He looks upon the women of his country as fruit in his vineyard, each worth a thousand pieces of silver. He considers her brothers the vineyard keepers, paying them two hundred pieces of silver for her. "But my own vineyard," she says, meaning her heart, "is mine to give." Thus she echoes her original speech, admonishing the Jerusalem daughters, women "that dwellest in the gardens,"[17] rather than the freedom of the fields.

As for her shepherd-lover, she can only bid him to flee from the enclosure of the city, back to the mountains where he at least can remain free.

Though this unusual book has been taken as an allegory, first by Jewish rabbis, for God and Israel, and later by Christian commentators as representing Christ and the Church, these scholars have had to ignore or bracket off the narrative portions that do not fit their interpretations. While there was a prophetic tradition symbolically comparing Israel to an unfaithful wife, the Song of Songs is a real love story. It rescues for us the delights of the sensual lost under layers of literary and theological notions about that original garden of delight—Eden. The eroticism of the Song of Songs is especially appealing to women. Never coarse, its exquisite metaphors are more imaginatively effective than the bald descriptions of sexual encounter we call "graphic" today.

Nevertheless, the story of these lovers is no happier than

the one of the two expelled from Eden. In fact, it illustrates one of the many ways our post-paradisal loves go wrong. The freedom of the fields and mountains is exchanged for the stifling enclosure of the harem. Power, privilege, and profit conspire to end the outdoor idyll of the Shulammite and her shepherd. The king himself is never directly blamed for the loss of their happiness, but the veiled language of metaphor allows criticism of royal prerogative, just as Shakespeare used it to reproach monarchs in his own day. The greedy appetite of the sovereign contrasts with the shepherd's single desire for the Shulammite. And her brothers, who sell their unruly sister, come off looking worst of all.

But despite the constraints of a culture that allowed her such little power over her own body, nevertheless the Shulammite maiden maintains a strong sense of her self. There is a place within her that she opens to no one except to those she chooses—the vineyard of her soul.

MARY OF BETHANY

Luke 10:38-42; John 11:1-46, 12:1-8; see also Matthew 26:6-13;
Mark 14:1-11; Luke 7:36-50

*U*nlike her sister Martha, an active, practical person, Mary of Bethany is quiet and introspective. Not the sort we would ordinarily call sensual. But there is more to Mary than first meets the eye. Though ordinarily she stays in the background, she is drawn irresistibly toward the man Jesus with an intensity found in no other person in the gospels.

In Luke's story about the two sisters, Mary never speaks, not even to defend herself from her sister's implicit charge of laziness. Her only act is in choosing. Otherwise she was passive. She sits at Jesus' feet and listens to his words. When her sister bustles in to point her accusing finger, Mary remains silent, allowing Jesus to speak for her.

The "good part," Jesus calls Mary's choice, "which shall not be taken away from her."[1] And we still have a hard time accepting that judgment. In order to protect that choice of Mary's, the Roman Catholic Church institutionalized the quiet stillness called contemplation by setting up communities of prayer. In the Protestant tradition, Mary's choice has an even harder time gaining acceptance, much less respect. Cultivation of the inner life, which requires sitting and listening, looks like loafing to those whose work-ethic often becomes a works theology. Yet this is not the only time Jesus defends Mary's choice.

The impractical, impulsive side of her nature shows again when her brother Lazarus dies and the mourning party from Jerusalem arrives at the sisters' home. Martha, hearing that Jesus is approaching, slips out of the house to warn him that potential enemies are there. But Mary thoughtlessly rushes out of the house to meet him, not stopping to consider the consequences for her Lord.

However, not all of the Jerusalem Jews who witness the raising of Lazarus react negatively. This unmistakable sign of Jesus' divine power, in fact, convinces some of them that he is the Messiah. Mary's impetuous rush to see Jesus was the catalyst that eventually brought them to belief.

Others who witness the miracle, though, hurry back to the religious officials in Jerusalem and report that this man is a worse threat than they had heretofore imagined. The marvel in Bethany sets in motion the plans to arrest Jesus.

Matthew and Mark both place the next Bethany scene at the home of someone called Simon the Leper, while John locates it at the sisters' home. Was Lazarus, like Peter, also called Simon? Had his death in fact been caused by leprosy, a disease that would require him to live outside the city, thus leaving the house in Martha's hands? Now that he was healed and could live at home again, did Matthew and Mark designate the house as his? Whatever the answer to those questions, it is obvious that neither of those two gospel writers was as familiar with the Bethany family as John. As if to clarify Matthew and Mark's account, John emphasizes that the Mary present at the raising of Lazarus is the same woman who plays a central role in this following scene.

Since Jesus intends to celebrate the Passover this year in Jerusalem, he decides to spend the next week at Martha's house in Bethany, only a few miles from the city. Martha is in the kitchen again, preparing a dinner both to honor her guest and celebrate her brother's restoration. And Mary has once more left her sister to do the work.

But this time she goes to unpack a secret treasure she's squirreled away for some special occasion—an entire pint of an expensive perfume. (Mark prices the contents of the alabaster container at three hundred denarii, almost a year's wages for a working man.) She slips into the dining room where the guests are reclining, assembled to celebrate her brother's new life. Approaching the couch where Jesus reclines, without a word of explanation she opens the vessel and pours it—all of it—over Jesus' feet. As the heavy scent rises, filling the room, the other people turn to stare. Then slowly, deliberately, Mary takes down her long hair and begins to wipe the feet of the man she loves above all others.

Throughout the entire scene, Mary never speaks. In fact, the only time Mary ever speaks is to echo her sister's words at her brother's tomb. Whereas Martha is never at a loss for words, Mary appears reticent in the extreme. She is forced to find other ways to express her devotion.

But Mary is proclaiming something more than simple emotion by this act. Her bizarre exhibition of love is much like the symbolic acts used by earlier Hebrew prophets to deliver their messages. Jeremiah used a rotten linen belt to illustrate his nation's decay; Mary is using her perfume to prophesy what lies ahead for Jesus. She sees what the others do not. Not much more than a week ago her brother came shuffling out of his tomb, grave clothes flapping around him. Another week and there will be another body, another tomb. She alone among Jesus' followers takes to heart his warnings about his approaching death.

Like most prophets, however, Mary and her message go unheeded. The other guests see only a woman with loose hair—something they understand easily enough. In fact, the disciples are outraged by Mary's behavior, finding it immodest, shocking—as well as an extravagant waste of the perfume.

"Shameful," they mutter amongst themselves. Judas, the treasurer of the group, voices what they're all thinking. "We could have done a lot of good with that. If she didn't need it, she could have given it to us. We'd have seen to it that the poor benefited from it at least."

Jesus, unperturbed by her act, speaks up immediately. "Just a minute here," he says. "Leave her alone. Don't you understand what this act of hers signifies? I'm going to die. And she's the only one who sees that. That's why she's used the perfume this way—to prepare me for burial." Then he points out the same thing to them he told Martha when she complained against her sister earlier. "There's nothing to stop you from doing what you want to. It's your choice. You can give to the poor anytime you want to. They're always there, ready and waiting for your charity. Me, on the other hand, you may not have around much longer."

Matthew extends Jesus' defense of Mary: "What she's done for me here is beautiful. Wherever my story is told she'll be a part of it. She'll never be forgotten." And indeed, Mary's story appears in all four gospels.

Mary remains in the background, except when her passion overwhelms her passivity. Her only means of expressing her inward ardor is aesthetic and symbolic. We *hear* Martha; we *see* Mary, her face veiled by her long hair as she wipes the perfume she's spilled on her Lord's feet. She *enacts* love; our memories are marked with the sight.

Jesus never upbraids anyone in the gospels for extravagance. In fact, he applauds it. He's all for generosity, never a utilitarian. In our culture, we tend to side with Judas. "She has done something beautiful for me," Jesus said. But what use is beauty? You can't eat it. It doesn't pay the bills. Yet it points beyond itself, in the direction of all our hungers.

When we grasp at beauty and try to possess it for ourselves, we become like Potiphar's wife, prisoners of sensuality. But when we allow our senses to aim us toward the source of beauty itself, we become like Mary—lavish with love.

Manipulative Women

Manipulative isn't a word we like to be called. We may admire the intelligence it implies, but we dislike the suggestion of meanness it carries. Owning up to deceit and stratagems shows us the worst side of women. Recently, I was disturbed to read the advice a Christian mother gave her daughter: "You have to know when to stop submitting and start outwitting." Only the servile need to manipulate others, we think.

True enough. But most of the world's women have indeed led lives of virtual, if not actual, servitude. Many women around the world today still do. Does that make their lives unimportant, their stories of no interest? Decidedly not. The Old Testament, in particular, seems unencumbered by our own culture's disdain for manipulation. The Hebrew tales present the shrewd maneuverings of their characters—both men and women—as cleverness, a way of outsmarting a more powerful adversary, rather than as a sign of weakness or servility.

In the New Testament we see a different attitude toward manipulation, however. In these stories, candor becomes the ideal way of dealing with conflict. Jesus himself is never manipulative—though his friends and followers sometimes wish he were a little less direct. In his dealings with the religious establishment, in particular, he is downright confrontational. Nor does he ever allow himself to be manipulated. He often requires people to state exactly what they want. And at his trial, he doesn't try to plea-bargain.

Which is not to say he doesn't practice indirection. His parables ambush us with the truth of human life. And in his conversations with individuals, many of them women, he patiently directs the discussion toward their deepest concern. Even with Salome, the mother of James and John, he strikes precisely the right note, neither trivializing her request nor patronizing her concern.

Servanthood, not servility, is the New Testament ideal. And manipulation a worn-out tool.

REBEKAH

Genesis 24, 25:19–26:11, 27

*T*he shadow of Sarah, Abraham's wife and the first Hebrew matriarch, falls across the story of Rebekah, the daughter-in-law she never knew. This strong-willed woman, who had conspired with her husband against pharaohs and kings, who had the audacity to laugh at angels, continued to exert her influence over her son Isaac even after her death. When he was still a child, she had been so jealous for his prerogatives, so fearful that Hagar's older boy might supplant him, that she had driven the slave woman and her child into the desert to die. Sarah had been fierce in her protection of Isaac; it was his father who had actually taken him up on Mount Moriah with the intention of making him a human sacrifice. Small wonder then that Isaac, still mourning his mother's death, remained unmarried at forty.

Sarah was already in her grave by the time Abraham sent his trusted steward back to northern Syria to find a wife for his son among his own people. Abraham, himself 140 years old, knew he might not survive till the steward returned from the long journey back to Padan-Aram on the far side of the Euphrates River.

"What if I can't find a woman willing to leave her family to come to this faroff land?" the steward asks, scrupulously trying to anticipate every contingency. He also realizes Abraham could die before his return.

"Whatever happens, don't let Isaac go back to my homeland. Canaan is the land that's been promised to us. He has to stay here, even if you can't find him a wife," Abraham tells him.

Isaac himself is never consulted about these arrangements. Abraham gives the steward complete power over his son's destiny. And indeed, Isaac plays an exceptionally passive role throughout his lifetime.

The steward, though he is not named in this section, may well have been Eliezer, the servant to whom Abraham had willed his property when he had despaired of ever fathering a child. And certainly the man discharges his duty in an exemplary way. When he arrives in Abraham's old hometown, his first stop is at the town well to water his ten camels. It is evening, the time when the women come to draw water. The steward prays to his master's God, asking for a sign that will reveal who among the women is the right one for Isaac. "If I ask her for a drink and she offers to draw water for my camels as well, that will be the right one."

Before he has even finished this prayer, Rebekah appears. She is beautiful, unspoken for, untouched. And when he asks her for a drink of water, as if on cue she offers to draw water for the camels as well. In fact, the story emphasizes her quickness to oblige. She runs between the well and the trough, filling it several times, since ten camels can drink a prodigious amount. The steward watches her, impressed. When she has finished, he rewards her labor handsomely with a gold nose ring and two gold bracelets. Then he inquires if there might be room at her father's house for him and the ten camels.

Rebekah, ever eager, assures him of a welcome at her home

and introduces herself in the customary way by sketching her familial connections. The steward is bowled over when he hears that she's actually his master's great-niece.

Rebekah runs home to tell her mother's household to prepare for a guest. When her brother Laban sees the expensive gifts the steward has already given his sister, he is eager to host this wealthy traveler. He hurries to the well to urge the steward to accept their hospitality.

In typical Middle Eastern fashion, a meal is spread before the steward, but, not wanting to profit from their generosity under false pretenses, he refuses to eat until he discloses his mission. Carefully crafting his message, he outlines Abraham's history since he left Haran many years ago, stressing how his wealth has grown; then he states his present mission—to find a wife for Abraham's son. He reports his prayer that the right girl be revealed to him that very day and the amazing way that prayer has been answered. "Now," he ends, "tell me how this strikes you. I need to know if you are open to my proposition before I take advantage of your hospitality."

Laban and his father practically fall over one another in their eagerness to give Rebekah to this ambassador from their wealthy relative. "Take her; she's yours," they say, adding, "this is obviously divine intervention. Who are we to stand in God's way?" No one, of course, asks Rebekah herself.

Next morning, the steward is anxious to be on his way with his prize. Laban and his mother try to cajole him into staying another week or so—Laban, no doubt, in the hope of extracting more gifts from this guest. But the steward insists he cannot tarry. He is anxious to return with Rebekah so that his master can see the success of his mission before he dies.

In order to stall a bit longer, they decide to ask Rebekah her preference, probably expecting that she would want time to prepare for the journey. Rebekah's reply no doubt surprised them all. "Let's go," she says, as eagerly as she offered to water the camels. So she and her maids mount their camels and follow this strange man from the fertile valleys of Mesopotamia southeast into the unknown.

It would have been many days and miles later before they spotted a man walking alone in a field. He looks up at the approaching caravan, shading his eyes. "Who's that?" Rebekah asks the steward.

"My master," he replies.

Immediately Rebekah makes her camel kneel and slides from the saddle, pulling her veil to cover her face. Her new master is there too, this man who will be her husband. Little did she know that he would prove so easy to manage.

Up to this point, every scene in this story has been presented dramatically, but the narrator draws a curtain across the culmination of this proxy love story. We are told that the two are married, that Isaac loves her, and strangest of all, that he brings her "into the tent of his mother Sarah,"[1] who is long since dead. Had Isaac kept the dwelling as a relic of his beloved mother? Was it a kind of shrine to him? Certainly it held some special meaning for him since this scene ends with the line: "and Isaac was comforted after his mother's death."[2] Rebekah has become the mother-substitute for her new husband. And among the matriarchs, she will be the only woman who does not have to compete with other wives.

That does not mean, however, that her life will be without shadows. For one thing, it takes her twenty years to get pregnant. Though that's considerably less waiting than her mother-in-law Sarah endured, for a Middle Eastern woman it was an interminable tribulation. So her husband Isaac appeals to the Lord on her behalf, and Rebekah finally conceives.

Then the trouble starts. There is such warfare in her womb that she goes to inquire of the Lord, probably from a local oracle, just what's happening within her. As the first woman in the Old Testament to take this task upon herself, Rebekah once more shows her initiative.

And the Lord answers her: "In your womb are two nations of people. One day they will be separated. One nation will be stronger than the other. It is the older who will serve the younger."

Sure enough, Rebekah delivers what at first appears to be a double blessing—twins. But even as infants the boys are very different. The first emerges red and hairy. The second is born with one hand gripping his brother's heel.

The first son they name Esau, or Red. The second is named Jacob, or Grabber. And the boys tend to live up to their names. Red is the outdoor type who spends his days hunting. His younger brother is described as "a quiet man"[3] and a homebody. Appreciating the company of women. A considerable consolation to his mother. Their father Isaac, on the other hand, who has an appetite for wild game, relishes the fruits of his older boy's hunting skill.

Jacob, whose own skills lie in the kitchen, is simmering a stew one day when his brother comes in from the chase, sweaty and hungry. "Give me some of that and be quick about it," he orders in a peremptory way. "I'm starving!"

Jacob, perhaps irritated by his big brother's lack of manners, decides to exact a price from the big lunk. "Fine," he replies, "I'll trade you the stew for your birthright."

"Sure, sure," Red says, brushing him aside. "I'm about to die anyway. What good would it do me then?"

But Jacob suddenly is not kidding. He means it. "Swear?" he says.

"Okay, okay. Just give me some." And Red grabs the stew from his brother, muttering something about who needs it anyway.

And now we see that Grabber lives up to his name. He has snatched from his brother the double portion of the wealth the older son would have inherited from their father. Strictly speaking, however, there has been no actual deception. It was a tradeoff—not exactly an even trade, but the terms were clearly stated.

Note that, so far, Rebekah has not been a part of this scheme. Though she is sometimes portrayed as the mastermind behind a conspiracy to supplant her older son with her own favorite, Jacob obviously has no trouble coming up with the idea all on his own.

When next we see the nomadic band, they have moved into the territory belonging to Abimelech, king of Gerar. Isaac had always shown tendencies to drift southward, toward Egypt, but now the Lord encourages him to stay in this region. In fact, he renews the same covenant he had earlier made with Abraham, telling Isaac he will make his descendants as numerous as the stars, a people who will become a blessing to all the nations of the earth. So Isaac stays put.

However, as children tend to do, he reenacts a scene from his own parents' past. Like Abraham, who had feared that the local inhabitants might get ideas about his beautiful wife and find an excuse to get rid of him so they could have her, Isaac shows a similar lack of backbone and spreads the same tale around Gerar—this woman is his sister, not his wife. (At least in Abraham's case, the statement was half true.) Just as before, however, the king discovers the truth. From an upper window he looks down and sees Isaac "sporting with"[4] Rebekah in an unbrotherly way. And again the king is perturbed by what the consequences might have been, though he allows the outlanders to go on living there, ordering special protection for Rebekah. Eventually, the nomads learn to plant crops, do well at it, and increase their wealth. Finally Abimelech insists Isaac's clan leave. "You're getting too powerful for us." So Isaac's entourage moves far enough away that life becomes temporarily peaceful.

But not for long. Esau, now forty, decides it's time to marry. And the local Hittite girls suit him fine. No sense sending away hundreds of miles for a bride when you can see what you're getting right there in Canaan. His parents may have disagreed about their two boys, but about these two daughters-in-law, Esau's wives, they were in complete accord— the two women gave them nothing but grief.

By now, Isaac is old—close to the century mark, in fact—

and blind as well. Sensing the end approaching, he knows it is time to give his eldest and favorite son his patriarchal blessing. He calls in Esau and says, "Son, get your bow and arrows and go rustle up some of that wild game you know I love so much. I may not have another chance to eat so well before I die. After I'm full, maybe I'll give you my blessing."

Now it just so happens that Rebekah is in the wings listening to this conversation. Knowing her husband's condition, she would be expecting this blessing ritual to take place soon. She hurries off to find her own favorite son. "Bring me two little goats from the flock. I can fix them so they'll taste like wild game—just the way your father likes it. Then you can serve it to him and get the blessing before your brother gets back."

Jacob hesitates. After all, he's already obtained Esau's double inheritance rights. Why should he care about the old man's blessing? "It'll never work," he tells his mother. "For one thing, my skin is smooth, not hairy like Esau's. As soon as Dad touches me, he'll know it's not Red. Then I'll really be in trouble. It won't be a blessing I'll get; he'll put a curse on me for trying to trick him."

Rebekah, however, is fully aware that the blessing is much more valuable than property. After all, God has personally promised her that her younger son, her own dear boy, is his choice too. That this sweet, sensitive baby of hers will end up dominating that big oaf Esau. "Not to worry," Rebekah assures Jacob. "I'll take care of everything. In fact, I'll stake my life on it. If the plan doesn't work, let your father's curse fall on me. Just do what I tell you. And be quick about it."

While Jacob is out separating two young kids from their mothers, Rebekah rummages through Esau's clothes and finds his best outfit. When Jacob returns she puts it on him and uses the skins from the goats to cover his neck and hands. After the meat is done, she hands him the platter, and he carries it in to his father, pretending to be Esau.

"Back from your hunting trip so soon? That was quick," Isaac says when he smells the steaming dish.

"Your God led me right to it—it was providential," Jacob responds piously.

The blind old man beckons. "Come closer, boy." He pats at the goatskin-covered cheeks and hands. "Hmm. Sounds like Jacob but feels like Esau. Is this really Red?"

"Of course."

"Okay then. Let me eat and then I'll bless you." Isaac finishes off the goat, wipes his mouth, and says again, "Come here, boy. Let me kiss you." Obviously, he's still not convinced this is his elder son. But when Jacob bends down to kiss his father, Isaac catches a whiff of Esau's pungent sweat from his clothes. Finally he's satisfied. "Ah yes. This is my son who always smells like the great outdoors." And thus deceived, Isaac bestows on his younger son the patriarchal blessing, an irrevocable act that gives him legal and spiritual power over his brother.

No sooner has Jacob grabbed the blessing rightfully belonging to his brother than Red appears, fresh from the hunt, thrusting his own steaming dish under his father's nose. But it's too late. The blessing has already been spoken, and no matter how loudly Esau protests, it cannot be recalled.

Esau, of course, is understandably infuriated with his younger brother. "Just wait," he mutters to himself. "Dad can't last much longer. As soon as he's in his grave, then I'll get that little wimp Grabber."

But Rebekah has her spies among the household servants, one of whom happens to hear these muttered threats and tells the mistress. As always, however, Rebekah takes the initiative. Jacob may be sharper than his big brother, but she knows he won't have a chance if it comes to a physical confrontation. After thinking it over, she decides she can now actually kill two birds with one stone. She has a new scheme whereby she can not only put the apple of her eye beyond the reach of his brother's murderous schemes but also ensure that he marries well.

Rebekah goes to her husband, who seems unaware of her part in the recent deception, and says with a heavy sigh, "You know, Isaac, life hasn't been worth living ever since Red married those Hittite floozies. What if Jacob does the same thing? I'll just die."

This speech has exactly the effect she intends. Right away Isaac calls Jacob in and orders him not to marry any of the local girls. "In fact," he says, "now that I think about it, the only thing for you to do is to go back to Padan-Aram to your Uncle Laban's. You can't find better women anywhere. That's where your mother came from, after all. Since you're now going to inherit the land God promised your grandfather Abraham, you need to get busy populating it."

So Jacob heads north, toward his mother's people and a land his father has never seen. Rebekah watches her darling go, glad he'll be out of harm's way, confident he will find a better wife among her own people than these dreadful Hittite women. The plan is unfolding, just as God promised before the boys were born. Like the younger son in fairy tales, her Jacob will turn out triumphant in the end, she's certain.

But there's a price to pay: Rebekah will never see her boy again.

Without question, Rebekah engineered this consummation of the plan. Without her conniving, Isaac would have done the customary thing—blessed the eldest son. Was Rebekah truly a manipulative woman, or merely expediting the outcome God had already announced to her during her tumultuous pregnancy?

Certainly she was a woman who never simply sat back and waited for things to happen, unlike her more passive husband. From the first time we see her at the well, she moves and acts with alacrity. But can deception of one's husband be justified by claiming partnership in divine planning?

The text offers no moral judgment of Rebekah's actions. She is neither condemned nor praised for scheming to supplant her older son with her own favorite. We only see the results—and that they were ordained long before her strategizing was conceived.

The entire saga of the patriarchs is full of tales of trickery, some instigated by men and some by women. Did the ancient Hebrews applaud the quality of shrewdness that allows the weak to win out over the strong? Did the original audience for this saga value the quiet Jacob who relied on his wits above the brute force of Esau? Certainly that pattern recurs often in the Old Testament. David and Goliath, Moses and Pharaoh, Elijah and Jezebel are only a few examples of stories that pit the weak against the powerful. Should Rebekah be stricken from the list? These are questions to ponder, while remaining cautious of hasty pronouncements based on our own cultural conditioning.

Yet despite our uncertainty as to proper judgment of this woman's actions, the one solid lesson we learn from Rebekah's story is that God often accomplishes his goals by unlikely means. As Rebekah's grandson Joseph will later explain to the brothers who sold him into slavery, "You intended evil, but God intended good."

DELILAH
Judges 16

*D*elilah is a woman of mystery. The facts we know are few: she lived in the Valley of Sorek during the time when Israel was ruled by judges—and became the lover of one of these, Samson. Though this most improbable "judge" had a weakness for women, she is the only one for whom the text supplies a name. Yet hers is a name to which no male kinship designation is attached— no "daughter of" or "wife of" or even "sister of"—a rarity in Scripture. We are not even certain of her nationality. The Valley of Sorek is near Samson's own hometown, though at this point in Israelite history, the loose confederation of the twelve tribes is under the domination of the coastal Philistines.

The only other woman to play such a decisive role in Samson's life is his mother. Before she even conceives, an angel appears to her, announcing that the son she will bear is to be consecrated to the Lord as a Nazirite. The angel gives her explicit instructions about what this means—no unclean meats, no wine, no haircuts.

A rather comic scene ensues in which the woman tells her

husband, Manoah, of the angel's visit, only to have him insist that the messenger return and repeat the instructions to him. The angel reappears all right, not to him but to his wife out in the field. She runs to find Manoah so that he can see this exotic personage for himself. The angel repeats his instructions—except for the detail about the haircuts—emphasizing that the woman is in charge of this project.

Manoah then wants to offer a burnt sacrifice to the messenger, but the angel tells him only God may receive such tribute. Then Manoah wants to know the stranger's name, supposedly to give him credit when his prediction comes true. The messenger tells him, however, that his name is too fantastic for Manoah's limited understanding. Still, Manoah insists on making the sacrifice, and only when he sees the angel ascending in the flames does he finally believe. "He really was from Heaven," he cries to his wife. "Oh no! We're going to die."

His wife very sensibly points out, however, that the Lord would hardly have given them the commission the angel delivered if he intended to strike them dead.

When their longhaired son grows up, he marries a Philistine woman. In an aside, the scriptural narrator points out that the Lord allows this to happen because he wants to stir up trouble with the Philistines; the Israelites had become complacent under their control. He certainly picked the right man in Samson, who loves a good brawl and, because of his amazing strength, always wins. The marriage ends when, infuriated with his father-in-law, Samson burns the crops of the Philistines who, in turn, burn down the father-in-law's house with the man and his daughter in it.

Instead of being stirred to revolt, however, the Israelites in the neighborhood are horrified. Knowing Samson's reputation, they come three thousand strong to arrest him and turn him over to the Philistines. He allows them to bind him and lead him before the enemy, but once he hears the taunts of the Philistines, he bursts the ropes and lays about him with a donkey's jawbone, killing a thousand of them.

Later he swaggers into Gaza, a Philistine stronghold, and avails himself of the services of a prostitute. When the Philistines are too frightened to attack him, he leaves her the next morning, taking the gates of the city with him.

As we can see, Samson is not exactly living the life one might expect of a judge. Certainly he is breaking almost every Nazarite rule there is. Drinking, brawling, consorting with prostitutes, he sounds more like an ancient version of a Clint Eastwood character than a holy man. About the only rule he hasn't broken so far is the no-haircut provision.

Then he meets Delilah, a woman who proves to be more than a match for him. She's no victimized weakling like his Philistine wife, but appears to have charge of her own household. Nor is her liaison with Samson a common commercial transaction as with the prostitute; the man is crazy about her.

Delilah has a head for business as well. Samson has proved too much for the Philistine warlords, who are now reduced to depending on a woman. They each offer Delilah eleven hundred pieces of silver (about twenty-eight pounds) if she can discover how to counteract the magic spell that gives this muscle-man his great strength. (This is one clue that Delilah may not be a Philistine herself since they do not appeal to her national loyalty.)

She begins her campaign at once. "Samson darling, tell me whatever makes you so big and strong. There must be some secret to such prowess as yours," she questions playfully.

And in the same spirit Samson teases her. "Just tie me up with seven fresh bowstrings that haven't yet dried and I'll be weak as a kitten."

So, with the Philistine warlords sequestered in her bedroom, Delilah ties Samson up with the bowstrings, then sits back. "Let's see if this works," she says. "Suppose your enemies the Philistines are attacking you now. What would you do?"

With a laugh, Samson pops the cords as if they were burnt thread.

Undiscouraged, Delilah puts on a pretty pout. "You old meany! You're just making fun of me. Now come on, Samson. Tell me your secret."

Still teasing, he tells her, "Okay. The real trick is to tie me up with new ropes—ones that no one has ever used before."

Like the bowstrings, acquiring such ropes takes little time, since she has the aid of her Philistine confederates. With them hidden once more in the bedroom, Delilah tries these on her lover. "Now see what you can do," she urges him. "Pretend the Philistines are coming to get you."

And to her chagrin, Samson again breaks the ropes as if they were mere thread.

Now Delilah alters her manner. "You're only making a fool of me with your lies," she tells him. "Now I'm serious—how can you be tied up?"

Figuring he's exhausted the rope-and-cord gambit, he invents a new subterfuge. "Here's what you do," he says. "See how my long hair is plaited into seven braids? Take them and work them into that weaving you're doing on your loom."

This time Delilah waits till he's asleep before she tries the trick. As he instructed, she weaves his seven braids into the web of her loom, fastens them tightly with the wooden beater, then cries out, "Samson, Samson, wake up! The Philistines are here!" (True enough, though Samson never catches onto that until it's too late.)

Startled from sleep, he leaps up and runs out, pulling the loom, weaving, beater, and all after him.

Now Delilah is really at her wit's end. She plays her final card, the old if-you-really-loved-me line. "You've tricked me three times," she complains. "You say your heart belongs to me, but I'm beginning to doubt it. How can you say you love me if you won't share your secret with me?"

Day after day she keeps up this line of attack. She wears him down until, as the Hebrew says literally, his soul was "shortened," and he reveals the secret he has guarded so carefully.

"If my long locks were ever cut off, then I'd be only as strong as any ordinary man."

Delilah sends word immediately to the Philistine warlords, who have no doubt grown tired of hiding in her closet. This time Delilah is confident—but canny. *Come quickly. He's told me his deepest secret.* But she doesn't tell them what the secret is. Not even when they arrive and hand over the silver they'd promised her.

Supposedly as a sign of how his trust has restored their intimacy, Delilah takes Samson to bed again. Then, while he is sleeping (some texts say "on," others "between" her knees), she has a man tiptoe in and cut off his seven long dreadlocks, the key to her doomed lover's might. She shakes him. "Wake up, Samson," she calls for the last time. "The Philistines have come for you."

Groggily Samson looks around, stumbles to his feet, staggers as the warlords seize him and drag him away from the house of the woman he has loved, not wisely but too well. His eyes are gouged out, and he is put to grinding grain for the Philistines down in Gaza, whose city gates he had confiscated after his night of carousing there.

Years go by. Samson's hair grows back. And one day when the Philistines are partying on a rooftop, celebrating a pagan festival, they call the blind man in to entertain them. Which he does with a vengeance. Wrapping his arms around the pillars that support the gallery, he brings the house down—literally—crushing three thousand Philistines along with himself. His final triumph. Which would never have happened without Delilah's part in this drama.

What becomes of Delilah? We never see her again after the warlords take her lover away. Supposedly she pockets the reward and lives happily ever after. The wrath of God doesn't fall on her for betraying Samson. The responsibility for his undoing is not shuffled off onto her. Her betrayal is part of the divine plan as much as Samson's earlier headstrong determination to marry a Philistine woman.

Of course, Delilah unwittingly cooperates with grace. Her motives are less admirable than Rebekah's, who was acting for the benefit of another and with knowledge of God's intentions for her sons. Nevertheless, Delilah's greed can be mitigated by her position as a woman alone. Being the mistress of an outlaw no doubt had its drawbacks. She was that rare creature in those primitive times, a woman who handled her own affairs without the intervention of a husband, brother, or son.

To her credit, Delilah never actually lies to Samson, although he repeatedly lies to her. She asks for exactly what she wants: the key to his supernatural strength. Undoubtedly she knew what had happened to Samson's bride, a woman he had made no effort to protect and did not mourn when she was incinerated.

The point of this story is not then, as it is often represented, the treachery of Delilah. Certainly she is no more reprehensible than her erstwhile lover. Rather, it shows us a cast of characters, none of them laudable with the exception of Samson's mother, who yet are used as God's instruments for accomplishing his design, slow though it may be in unfolding.

SALOME, WIFE OF ZEBEDEE
Matthew 20:20-28, 27:56; Mark 15:40-41, 16:1-8

*J*esus calls two sets of brothers as his first followers. Mark has it that Simon (later called Peter) and Andrew are at work, casting their fishing nets, when Jesus summons them, promising them a different kind of catch. Mark emphasizes they left their *nets*, their means of livelihood, to follow this new rabbi.

Luke's gospel adds that James and John, the sons of Zebedee, were business partners of Simon Peter. Jesus calls this pair of brothers next. Mark emphasizes these two leave their *father* in the boat, stressing their sacrifice of family ties.

They may have left their father, Zebedee, but not their mother, Salome. She is one of the women, mentioned in all three synoptic gospels, who "followed Jesus from Galilee, ministering unto him."[1] Very likely Zebedee was already furious when the boys he'd raised and trained in his trade left him to follow some wandering rabbi. And his temper would not improve when his wife traipsed after the same madman.

Interestingly, once Salome becomes a follower of Jesus,

she is never again referred to as Zebedee's wife but either by her own name or as "the mother of Zebedee's children."[2] The latter identification suggests that her husband may have divorced her for her scandalous behavior. Her renunciation of the social position, security, and protection Zebedee provided was even greater than her boys' sacrifice, though it is seldom remarked upon.

After they leave home, Jesus nicknames her sons the Boanerges Boys—equivalent to something like Sons of Rage. Was this epithet an allusion to their father's fiery temperament or to their own irascibility? We see them both react with rash violence later. John, for instance, orders a man to stop using Jesus' name to drive out demons because he doesn't belong to their team. On another occasion James and John offer to call down fire from Heaven to destroy a Samaritan village that gave them a chilly reception. Both times Jesus rebukes their smug censure and unwarranted ferocity.

Salome, however, loves her boys, unruly though they are. And, when Jesus takes them into his inner circle along with their old fishing partner Peter, she is understandably proud. After all, they have given up everything to follow this Messiah-in-the-Making. Salome has complete confidence that Jesus will soon be riding into Jerusalem as a conquering hero, ready to take over the government from corrupt politicians and petty religious bureaucrats who make life hard for working people with their burdensome ceremonial requirements. When *their* Messiah takes over, they won't be outsiders anymore. Her misconception of Jesus' mission was, of course, no different from that of his male disciples. Primarily blue-collar workers, they both resent and envy the white-collar Jews of Jerusalem.

Like a rich yuppie who comes to consult the rabbi about his spiritual destiny one day. When the wealthy young man can't bring himself to turn over his substantial investments to the poor and join their band, the disciples are not surprised. What does surprise them is Jesus' remark about wealth being a hindrance to seeking God. Doesn't it take money to keep kosher and make frequent temple sacrifices to get off the hook with God? But Jesus tells them it's the rich people who are burdened—with their own possessions. "They can't get through the narrow gate to God because of the pack on their backs," he says.

Peter catches on—sort of. "All right!" he exclaims, rubbing his hands together. "We've got it made then. We've certainly thrown away our excess baggage. We've left everything behind." Then he strokes his chin, pondering. "The way I figure it, we're due for a reward once you get to be king, right?"

"Let me assure you," says Jesus, "your sacrifices won't go unnoticed. Once I'm ruling after the restoration, you'll sit on thrones as well—twelve of them—judging the chosen people of God."

It's easy enough for us to see, with two thousand years of hindsight, what Jesus meant. But it's also easy to understand how this statement could be misinterpreted, especially by ears eager to hear another message. In fact, the disciples are so intent on this promise of power that they miss the warning Jesus attaches to his pledge: "But many that are first shall be last; and the last shall be first."[3]

Sensing that this final point hasn't sunk in, Jesus tells them a parable, the one about the workers in the vineyard, the kicker being that the field hands who were hired late in the day got the same pay as those who'd been slaving away since sunup. Again, he underscores the point for them with the same warning: "So the last shall be first, and the first last."[4] Did they get it? Or did they think he was pointing the finger at those Jerusalem fat cats, saying their days were numbered, that Jesus' own motley band of backwater Galileans were going to take over and replace them soon?

Salome heard both the parable and the warning, too. However, she understood it much as Peter did—they were the last, the least, who were about to be elevated to positions of power.

When Jesus got to be king, they'd be in on the ground floor of a new political regime.

So while the convoy is on its final approach to Jerusalem, Jesus tries one more time to imprint on their minds the paradox of a suffering savior, a desecrated deliverer. Since the twelve thrones he mentioned earlier seem to have stirred up their dreams of power, he pulls the twelve men aside to make his point even plainer to them. "Look," he says, "We'll be in Jerusalem soon. I can assure you the head honchos there are not going to be impressed with me as the model of mankind. In fact, you should expect just the opposite. They'll plot against me, convincing the Romans I'm a threat to the national security. I'll end up a laughingstock—not a hero but a fool. And a dead one at that. But the third day I'll come back."

Why aren't the women included in this huddle? Perhaps because Jesus knows they have no illusion about gaining political power for themselves. It simply isn't within their cultural expectations to claim a throne, no matter how much they have given up to follow the rabbi. Nevertheless, even stronger than the personal ambition that motivates the men of the company is the maternal instinct of at least one woman—Salome. She has not heard Jesus' description of what they could expect in Jerusalem. So she comes to him, falling on her knees as if petitioning a king.

"What do you want?" he asks, his standard response to all suppliants, one that forces them to focus and clarify their desires.

And Salome has no difficulty coming right out with it. She doesn't beat around the bush, hinting as Peter did, about all her boys have sacrificed for him. She is stunningly blunt: "When you get to be king, give my two sons the thrones on either side of you, one on the right hand, and the other on the left."

Were the Sons of Rage embarrassed by their mother's request? Mark's gospel has James and John make the request themselves, which perhaps indicates they too thought they should receive positions of honor. Jesus acknowledges this as their own desire by responding directly to Salome's sons. "You don't know what you're asking for." Then he tells them—one more time—what such a role will mean. "Can you endure what I'm going to have to undergo?"

"Sure," the sons say, eager to get their commissions.

A squabble breaks out now because the other ten men are angry with James and John for being so pushy.

"Let's try this one more time," Jesus says, trying to calm them down. "My rule isn't like the Romans'. They like to flex their muscles, flaunt their power over others. But under my administration, the rulers will actually be those who minister to others; they'll be the servants."

Many commentators want to write Salome out of the script altogether because Jesus shifts his focus from her to her sons. Even the recent *Women's Bible Commentary* says Jesus "repudiates the woman by addressing his response directly to the disciples, and he repudiates her agenda by emphasizing service, not supremacy." But this is not what he's doing. He deflects the brunt of his reproach from the mother to her sons, first, because he means it for them.

Salome is not the one trying to be first. She is asking on behalf of the two sons she loves. Jesus' admonition falls precisely on those for whom he intends it—those who want to be at the top of the totem pole—and there are plenty of contenders for that spot.

Nevertheless, his shift in attention carries a message for Salome also. She has not answered his question with what *she* wants but with her sons' desires. If she continues to live her life solely through her children, then her personal significance will be lost in the shuffle. Yet Jesus also confirms that the work she's been doing—ministering—is exactly the labor that makes one great. Salome and the other Galilean women have been "ministering unto" him. Now he uses the same word to admonish his male disciples about the business they should be about. It is the same word used for the angels who "ministered" to

Jesus after his temptation in the wilderness—and that Jesus uses to describe his own mission. When they serve as he does—and as the women in their band do—they're already great in the Kingdom.

This remains the most difficult message of all for Jesus' band to hear and assimilate. Men still squabble over positions of power in the church and debate who is worthy to sit on the "thrones." Meanwhile, women still do most of the actual work of ministering—raising funds, caring for the sick, keeping people fed and clothed. The same kind of work that makes us like God. Work that, for the most part, either goes unrecognized or is patronized.

Many kinds of activity are called "ministry" today, whereas people in Salome's day were pretty clear that it was the work servants did, waiters in particular. Who serves the potluck dinners and cleans up afterward in your church? How many members—men or women—are contending for that honor? When you're scraping greasy plates—or sitting up with a sick child—you feel it wouldn't be so bad if the job were really valued by others. If you could just get a little appreciation for it. No doubt God feels the same way.

But whatever we're feeling—oppression, resentment, or even a fleeting and almost guilty satisfaction with our work—the trick is to answer truthfully that insistent question of Salome's rabbi: "What do *you* want?" If we try to hide our own desires behind those of others, even those we love, Jesus will not answer us directly. Only when we come face to face with our own desire for power can we escape the deadly loop of maneuvering for first place.

Political Women

Politics, strictly speaking, is the exercise of power. Bismarck, known as the Iron Chancellor of Germany, added that politics is "the art of the possible," emphasizing that no one, not even the most unrestrained emperor, can do absolutely as he pleases but must at some point make compromises.

Women of the ancient world had precious little power to exercise, at least in the arena of public affairs. In domestic situations, where personal authority weighs more heavily, they had a good deal more influence, as the stories of Sarah and Rebekah demonstrate. Nevertheless, some notable women attained positions through which they affected the course of their nations' history.

No subjects of ancient kingdoms, men or women, possessed the kind of political power citizens in modern democracies do. All the societies described in the Bible—except for the nomadic tribes and the brief period when judges directed Israel—were monarchies, some more structured than others. Thus, political power belonged almost exclusively to the king and his court.

But even kings have families, and since most monarchies are hereditary, the women married to rulers often used their position as leverage. Sometimes a forceful woman like Jezebel or Herodias relished power for its own sake. But a woman like Esther, though it jeopardized her own life, controlled the rash decrees of her intemperate consort for the good of her entire people.

ESTHER

Esther 1–10

*E*very year in late winter Jews celebrate the Feast of Purim, or the Day of Dice. This holiday dates back roughly twenty-five hundred years, when the Persians dominated the entire Middle East, from India to Egypt. Though many Jews had been deported from their homeland in Palestine generations earlier by the Babylonians, they clung stubbornly to their national identity while at the same time adapting to life in foreign lands.

Esther is an orphan who has been reared by her older cousin Mordecai. Both these names are Babylonian (the culture that developed astronomy), and refer to the planets Venus and Mars, respectively. As part of their cultural adaptation, most Jews acquired new names taken from their captors' vocabularies. Esther's Jewish name was Hadassah, one she probably used only with Mordecai, since he instructs her to conceal her Jewish identity.

Jewish literature frequently gives Hebrew names to foreigners also, especially kings—the exile's subtle revenge, perhaps. Xerxes, the Persian king (486–465 BC), is called

Ahasuerus in this book. Ahasuerus was a man who relished the power of his position. He burned Athens; he destroyed the Babylonian temples, melting down their idols for the gold; he plundered the temple treasures of Egypt to enlarge his own collection of diverse drinking cups. These diplomatic indiscretions gained him no friends abroad. And the same intemperate behavior at home makes him a comic character in this story.

The book opens with a feast the king hosts to show off the splendor of his new winter palace in Susa. Toward the end of the feast, when the king and his guests are roaring drunk, Ahasuerus calls for his beautiful wife, Queen Vashti, to come to the banquet hall and expose her physical attractions to his guests, no doubt to further inflame their envy.

The queen, who is herself holding a banquet for the wives of the visiting dignitaries, refuses to come. Ahasuerus is furious. She's humiliated him in front of the visiting potentates. One of the provincial satraps speaks up: "It's not only you she's insulted, my lord. Vashti has injured us as well. Wait till our wives hear about this! Every woman in the kingdom will be thumbing her nose at her husband. We'll all lose control!"

So Ahasuerus consults with his grand viziers. How should Vashti be punished? After much consideration, they come up with this penalty: Vashti will never again be allowed to come before the king, and her estate will go to her replacement. In addition, in order to satisfy the wounded pride of his guests—and save face himself—the king sends out a decree, phrased in a comically grandiose manner, that all wives everywhere, both great and small, are to respect their husbands.

Diaspora Jews would have viewed the pompous bombast of this first scene as a lampoon of the great Persian Empire using its awesome political power to quell an insurrection among its womenfolk.

The second scene opens with Ahasuerus suddenly realizing as his ire cools that he can't see the beautiful Vashti anymore. So, in good fairy-tale fashion, he stages a competition to find the most beautiful woman in the kingdom. The lucky winner will become his new queen. From every province of the empire women come to the winter palace where they are put into the care of Hegai, the eunuch in charge of the royal harem. He is instructed to give them beauty treatments for a year—six months using oil of myrrh and six months of aromatherapy.

Mordecai sees the beauty contest as a good career move for his ward, Esther, and brings her to the palace. Hegai takes a shine to her immediately and makes her his special project, taking personal charge of her wardrobe and makeup. The next step in the competition works like this: every night Hegai takes a new contestant to the king. The next morning, she goes to "the second house"[1] where, unless the king calls for her again, she will live out the rest of her life as a reject among his concubines.

But, thanks to Hegai's special coaching, Esther is clearly the odds-on favorite for queen. When it's her time for an interview with the king, Hegai dresses her carefully. And the king is bowled over. "This is the one!" he cries as soon as he sees her and immediately puts Vashti's crown on her head. At the wedding feast, swept away by emotion, Ahasuerus showers everyone with gifts and proclaims a tax cut for the provinces.

In the meantime, Mordecai, himself a member of the Susa Chamber of Commerce, happens to overhear two disgruntled bodyguards plotting the king's assassination. Mordecai reports this to Esther, who tells the king. The bodyguards are executed, and Mordecai is recorded in the government archives as a national hero.

In the next scene the villain of the story makes his appearance—Haman, a man recently promoted by the king to his second in command. All the other courtiers and leading citizens, anxious to secure Haman's good offices, bow and scrape when he passes. All except Mordecai. Being a Jew, he cannot bow down to another mortal. That honor belongs only to God. Comments about Mordecai's behavior get back to Haman, who is enraged that anyone would fail to properly appreciate his position. When he discovers that Mordecai refuses to kneel to him on religious grounds, Haman determines his revenge will not be on Mordecai alone but on all such uppity Jews.

Haman goes to the king and reports that a certain class of immigrants among his people live by a different set of laws than the rest of his subjects, laws that tend to undermine the king's authority. "Such people ought to be hunted down and exterminated," he says. "I'll personally put up three hundred seventy-five tons of silver as bounty money for these traitors."

At that offer the king's eyes light up. "Fine," he says, "I'm putting you in charge of the whole operation."

To determine the most propitious date for his pogrom, Haman throws the *purim*, or dice. They come up with the thirteenth day of Adar, the last month of the year. So he sends out a decree to the provinces, sealed with the king's ring, commanding all patriotic Persians on that day to rise up against their Jewish neighbors and kill them. All of them, including old people, women, and children.

When Mordecai hears the news he is horror-stricken, as are all Jews everywhere in the kingdom. Mordecai smuggles a copy of the decree to Queen Esther in the palace harem, along with the message that she should plead with the king to rescind this cruel edict.

But Esther has a problem. The king doesn't like to be disturbed. No one visits him in his private quarters without an invitation. Anyone who presumes to intrude is courting death. If the king's in a good mood, he will hold out his golden scepter as a sign of favor. But if he's not feeling particularly sociable— watch out!

She sends a message to Mordecai, explaining this complication. "The king hasn't asked to see me in a month now. I have no idea how he might respond to my sudden appearance."

Desperately, Mordecai replies to his protégé: "You can't think of yourself at a time like this. Our people's future is riding on you. You won't escape either. Someone's bound to find out your ethnic background and turn you in. Your position will be no protection against this decree. If you keep silent now, another deliverer will be provided, but your family name will be destroyed. Who knows? Maybe you were chosen in the beauty contest just so you'd be able to save your people now."

Esther responds to this challenge in truly regal manner. She sends a message to her cousin to pass the word among all the Jews in the city to fast for her for three days, during which time she and her maids will also fast. "At the end of that period, I will approach the king, even though he has forbidden it," she tells him. "And if I perish, I perish."[2]

After three days of fasting, Esther prepares for the dramatic confrontation. She knows Ahasuerus is subject to imperious caprice. After all, look what happened to her predecessor. Nevertheless, she dresses in her queen's robes and glides into the inner court where the king is sitting on his throne. He glances up and sees her, stares—then stretches out his golden scepter to her.

She must have been quite a vision. Not only has she overcome Ahasuerus' dictum against being disturbed, but he is so pleased to see her that he promises to give her anything she asks for—up to half his kingdom.

But Esther proceeds cautiously. She makes no request at this time, only tenders an invitation. She's giving a little cocktail party that evening, she says, and would like him and his buddy Haman to come.

"Count on it," he says.

That evening with Haman in tow, the king asks again what he can do for her. She responds again by inviting them to another party the next day. "I'll let you know my request then."

Haman leaves the cocktail party thrilled at the invitation from the queen. As he's going out the gate, he happens to pass

Mordecai, who merely gives him a steely look instead of drop-ping to his knees the way the other minions do. This damp-ens Haman's spirits momentarily, but he hurries home to tell his wife how his stock has soared at the palace. Not only has he been promoted, but the queen's invitation to her private party with the king has put him on the social register.

Then he sighs heavily. "There's only one fly in the oint-ment—that Jew, Mordecai. He's spoiling my triumph."

His wife comes up with a remedy immediately. "Build a seventy-five-foot-high gallows," she advises, "and first thing tomorrow, get the king's permission to hang Mordecai. Then you'll be in better spirits for going to the queen's dinner party."

Meanwhile, back at the palace, the king is having trouble sleeping. So he tells his valet to bring his favorite book, *The Adventures of Ahasuerus, King of Persia,* and read him a bed-time story. As it happens, the book falls open to the account of how Mordecai foiled the assassination plot against the king by his bodyguards.

"Hmm," muses Ahasuerus, stroking his beard. "Did I ever do anything for Mordecai? Reward him in any way?"

"No, your majesty."

"Well, we'll have to remedy that. Is anyone still in the office tonight?"

As it happens, Haman, impatient to put his own plot into operation, has returned to the palace to ask for permission to hang Mordecai. He is quickly ushered into the king's bed-room.

"Suppose I wanted to honor someone," the king asks him speculatively. "How should I go about it?"

Naturally Haman thinks the king means him, so he piles on all the sumptuous suggestions he can come up with—royal robes, a parade through the streets on a thoroughbred horse, with one of the royal princes acting as herald proclaiming him as the king's favorite.

"Great!" Ahasuerus agrees. "I knew I could count on you. Now then, see that your plan is carried out. And by the way, the man on the horse? That'll be Mordecai."

When Haman tells his wife that his plan has not only failed but backfired, she shakes her head. "I hate to say this, honey, but it looks like this Mordecai has got the jump on you. Why do I get the feeling you're not going to win this one?"

At the dinner party the next day, while Esther and her guests are reclining on their couches around the buffet table, Ahasuerus renews his promise to give his queen whatever she wants—up to half his kingdom.

"All I want," she finally tells him, "is to be allowed to live. Maybe you don't know, but I and my people have been sold—and not just into slavery. We've lived through that before and we could do it again. But our enemy has sold us to be slaughtered like animals."

"What? Who are you talking about?" the king exclaims. "Who would dare threaten my queen?"

Esther turns and points at Haman. "There he is." And Haman's frightened grimace gives away his guilt.

Ahasuerus is furious. He springs up from his couch and stalks out into the palace garden to calm down. But if the king is upset, think how Haman feels. He scrambles to his feet and rushes to Esther, begging her to save him from the king's wrath. When she ignores his pleas, he collapses in despair onto her couch.

At that moment the king reappears in the doorway. "What?" he bellows. "Now you're trying to rape my wife? And me right in the house? I've had enough. Guards, take him away."

So Haman is dragged out and hanged on the very gallows he had prepared for Mordecai. And the man he had built it for is elevated by the king to fill Haman's vacant position as second in command.

Troubles are not over for the Jews, however. The decree that Haman had instigated earlier, ordering their extermination, still stands. And according to Persian law, any provision the king has set his seal to is irrevocable. Even the king himself cannot countermand his own royal edicts.

Esther appeals to him once more, this time in tears. "How can I stand to see my people destroyed?" she said. "I won't be able to endure it."

So Ahasuerus commissions Mordecai to write a second edict and send it throughout the provinces, this one giving Jews the right to raise a militia and defend themselves from anyone trying to attack them on the day appointed for the pogrom. Not only that, but they will be allowed to avenge themselves on their enemies. Thus the story ends with a good deal of gore—several hundred enemies of the Jews are killed in Susa alone, including the ten sons of Haman.

Finally, in order that this grand reversal of fortune might not be forgotten, Queen Esther herself writes to all Jews scattered throughout every village of the empire, establishing the Feast of Purim as a perpetual remembrance of their deliverance. Supposedly, she and cousin Mordecai lived long and prospered. As for Ahasuerus, though the event is not recorded in this story, history records that he was murdered in his bed.

The book of Esther was written for, and probably by, Jews who managed to survive among strangers only by exercising their wits. Esther is a model of how exiles, by capitalizing on their assets and exercising prudence, may survive in constricted circumstances. In other words, the art of the possible.

Women in the Bible often find themselves in less-than-ideal situations. Rahab was a prostitute, Rizpah a cast-off concubine. Yet despite those unsavory situations, their lives gained meaning because they seized whatever opportunity presented itself and acted.

We tend to be priggish today about women using their good looks to gain power. But both as a woman and an exile, Esther was in a position of weakness. And when an avenue to power opened to her she did not disdain it. Nevertheless, it was a power she used, not for her own aggrandizement, but to protect her people.

JEZEBEL

1 Kings 16:29–19:18; 21; 2 Kings 9

*P*olitical power in ancient Israel was never very stable. When the twelve tribes entered the Promised Land after their long wandering in the desert, they operated for several hundred years under a loose confederacy, relying on judges to settle disputes between groups and individuals. Sometimes the need arose for such leaders to serve for a time as military commanders as well. This remarkably unstructured form of government, however, not only left the people vulnerable to attacks from hostile neighbors but also laid a burden of personal freedom on their shoulders they were not prepared to carry. The book of Judges ends with these words: "In those days there was no king in Israel: every man did that which was right in his own eyes."[1] A situation our own society might perceive as ideal.

However, the nations that encircled the Israelites were better organized. They had kings—though the kingdoms sometimes consisted of little more than a single walled city and its surrounding farmland. Having a king tended to centralize, and thus stabilize, the government. It also meant having a standing army, better police protection. Thus the Israelites eventually opted for a monarchy themselves, despite the warnings of the prophet Samuel that a king would impose burdensome taxation and the draft—for both men and women.

Israel never really took to monarchical government. For one thing, monarchies are usually hereditary, whereas Israel had always relied on the hand of Providence to appoint—and anoint—leaders. Thus Israel's kings, starting with Saul, the first one, were always vulnerable to military coups. But perhaps more importantly, Israel had a higher authority than even the king, one that reached farther back into its history—the Law. While other Middle Eastern monarchs could operate despotically, in Israel no man superseded the Law, not even the king. Kings were mortal; the Torah was eternal. It served as Israel's hedge against absolute tyranny, providing legal protections to every citizen not even the king could disregard.

It is this aspect of Israelite politics that Jezebel never understands. She has grown up in the royal household of Sidon, a city on the Mediterranean coast south of what is now Beirut. As king, her father wields absolute power. When she marries Ahab, son of Israel's king Omri, she fully expects to exercise the same kind of power there that she formerly enjoyed in Sidon.

Jezebel has also grown up in a very religious household. Besides king, her father is also a priest of Baal, the Palestinian fertility god.[2] Introduced into Israelite society generations earlier by some of Solomon's wives, Baal cults already flourish in her new kingdom. Her husband Ahab, a dabbler in Baal-worship himself, offers no objection when Jezebel imports her own favorite goddess Astarte, the female consort to Baal.

For obvious reasons, fertility deities most often came in pairs. Their worship included the physical reenactment of the gods' cosmic coupling, which supposedly brought fruitfulness to fields and flocks. Astarte's temples were stocked with priestesses who played the part of the goddess, receiving the seminal offering of male worshipers—who were expected to make cash donations as well. In special emergencies or community disasters, these gods required the sacrifice of children, often by burning.

Jezebel finds her father-in-law Omri to be quite an able leader, at least militarily. A hundred years after his death the Assyrians still called Israel "the land of Omri." He also built Samaria, the new capital of Israel. Ahab and Jezebel live in the palace he erected there, but Jezebel can see that Omri's son fails to live up to his father's mark. Soon Jezebel is setting the tone for Ahab's kingdom, one based on luxurious self-indulgence, and sacralized eroticism.

But she overlooks Elijah, the champion God has chosen to combat the Astarte invasion. And the Lord couldn't have picked a less appealing fellow—uncouth, crabby, and often cowardly. If time worked backward, Elijah could have come straight from the pages of a Flannery O'Connor novel. Like John the Baptist in a later age, Elijah lives in the wilderness on a diet that would gag most people—bread scraps and road-kill regurgitated from ravens' mouths, morning and evening. While hired prophets are swilling wine back in the palace, Elijah drinks runoff in the wadi.

Then a drought settles over the land. Israelites may have been copulating religiously at Astarte's temple, but the promised fruitful fields have not materialized. Just the opposite, in fact. Because no rain falls to water the crops, the country is facing famine. Soon there's not even ditchwater for Elijah to drink. So the Lord sends him—of all places—to Sidon, Jezebel's homeland. When Elijah reaches the village of Zarephath, he notices a poor widow gathering sticks for a fire and asks her for a drink of water, then something to eat.

"Look," she tells him, obviously astounded by his audacity, "I'm down to my last handful of flour myself. I was going to fix a little bread for me and my son to eat before we die."

This is just the woman the Lord is looking for—someone who's literally scraping the bottom of the barrel. "Use that last handful of flour for me," Elijah challenges her, "and

I promise you won't run out of food again as long as the famine lasts."

The woman shrugs. What have I got to lose, she figures, and cooks what she fears will be their last supper. But no! When she looks, there *is* more flour in the bottom of the barrel, just as the prophet promised.

Elijah and the widow ride out the famine together there in Sidon until one day the woman's son falls deathly ill. As the boy is breathing his last, she turns on Elijah. "Why did I ever get mixed up with you?" she cries. "Did you only come here to make me pay for my sin with my son's life?" Remember that this woman is a Sidonian, not an Israelite. All her life she's worshiped Baal and Astarte. And she's used to the notion that gods sometimes demand one's child as a sacrifice.

Elijah carries the boy's limp body upstairs to his room and lays it on the bed. First he upbraids the Lord for violating this woman's hospitality. Then he begins to plead for the boy's life. And amazingly, the child revives. When the prophet carries the boy back to his mother, she is overwhelmed, praising both Elijah and the power of his God.

Why is this nameless woman introduced in the middle of Jezebel's story? Because the widow's extreme poverty and remarkable graciousness toward Elijah serve as a foil to the queen's opulence and arrogance. Though the widow comes from the same Sidonian culture as Jezebel, she is able to transcend that background and grasp the Living God. She is not culturally bound. Even the women who worship Jezebel's goddess can escape their own degradation and the destruction of their children when their hearts are open.

Jezebel's, however, is decidedly closed. So is her mind. Not content with importing her own Astarte cult into Israel, she now intends to stamp out rival religions, especially that of Yahweh, the Living God. To that end, she has ordered the summary execution of all prophets of Yahweh.[3] The royal butler, Obadiah, has managed to save a hundred such men by hiding them in a cave and smuggling bread and water to them.

Meanwhile, the famine grows worse. There has been no rain for three years now. When Ahab sends Obadiah out to search the countryside for grass to feed the horses in the royal stables, the butler comes upon Elijah returning from Sidon.

"Just the fellow I wanted to see," Elijah greets him. "I need you to bring the king out to meet with me."

"Sure," Obadiah says, "like I'll just tell the king that Elijah wants to have a little chat. You're a wanted man, you know. The king's been looking for you for three years now. He holds you responsible for this drought. Besides, I know what'll happen. As soon as I turn my back the Lord will blow up a big wind and whisk you off someplace else. By the time I get the king out here, you'll be gone. You think I'm crazy? Look. It's not like I'm not on your side. I hid a hundred of those Yahweh-prophets and kept them alive while Jezebel was trying to kill them. You may as well go ahead and finish me off now, instead of setting me up like this. He'll kill me if he gets here and you're gone."

"Don't worry. I'll be here," Elijah assures him. "I promise."

So Obadiah brings Ahab out to meet with Elijah. "Aha," the king says when he sees the prophet, "you're back to stir up more trouble, I see."

"I'm not the troublemaker here," Elijah counters. "You're the one who turned your back on the Law and took up with your wife's gods. But I have a plan. I want you to send for those 450 prophets who serve Baal and those 400 Astarte priests Jezebel feeds. Have them come to Mount Carmel. And tell all the people to come too. It's going to be quite a show."

Ahab is so desperate to end the famine at this point that he complies. The people and prophets assemble at Mount Carmel, a high hill near the border of Sidon. From that promontory Elijah makes a speech to the people. And as usual, he's not very diplomatic. "Why can't you Israelites make up your minds? If Yahweh's in charge, then follow him. If Baal's in control, then make him your only god."

But his challenge meets with nothing but silence.

"Fine," Elijah says. "It looks like I'm the only one left willing to stand up for the Living God while Baal has 450 men backing him. But I've arranged a little scientific experiment here. I've got two bulls, one for them and one for me. We're going to cut up the carcasses and lay the pieces on some firewood I've brought. Then we'll see which god can light a fire under this barbecue."

Not surprisingly, despite their frenzied dancing around the sacrifice for hours, the prophets of Baal can't light a spark. Rubbing their nose in their failure, Elijah thoroughly soaks both his firewood and the carcass. With a flash, it goes up in smoke. The people begin to cheer and chant "Yahweh is God, Yahweh is God"—which in Hebrew sounds much like Elijah's own name. Then they lead the defeated Baal-prophets off to their execution.

The prophet's next assignment is to break the three-year drought. Hearing the rumble of thunder in the distance, Elijah tells Ahab to get ready for a downpour. Then he prays: "Please, God, send the people rain." Finally a small cloud can be seen out over the sea. It grows, darkening as it heads toward land.

"This is it," Elijah tells the king, "the rain you've been waiting for. You better get your chariot down off this mountain pronto so you won't get stuck. It's going to be a gully-washer!" Ahab, for once, listens to the prophet and heads back to the Pass of Jezreel.

Elijah is ecstatic. *I'm on a roll now*, he thinks, and hitching up his skirts, runs all the way to the mountain pass, beating Ahab's chariot there.

Meanwhile back at the palace, Jezebel has heard about the massacre of her Baal-prophets, and she's furious. The results of the contest have impressed her not a whit. She sends word to Elijah: "You can bet your bottom shekel that before another day passes you'll be in the same shape as my slaughtered prophets."

So Elijah takes off running again, this time in a different

direction. Knowing Jezebel to be a woman of her word, he takes his bodyguard and heads south, skirting the capital. He doesn't stop till he reaches the Negev desert where he holes up in a cave.

Jezebel's temper is not improved when the prophet slips through her hands a second time. Her husband Ahab is not in a good mood either. *Maybe I should encourage him to take up a hobby*, she thinks, *something that would take his mind off all these complicated matters of state*. A little gardening perhaps. Wholesome recreation, fresh air, exercise. That should improve his spirits.

From the palace high on the hill of Samaria the royal couple can look down into the fertile valley of Jezreel, full of vineyards, flourishing now that the drought has ended. Spotting a likely one, Ahab goes down to negotiate a price for the vineyard adjoining his palace property. But Naboth, the owner, isn't interested in selling. "Look," Ahab tells him, "I'm willing to pay a fair price. Or even make a trade, if that's what you want."

"Sorry," Naboth says, refusing to budge, "but it's not a matter of money. This property's been in the family since the Lord divided up the Promised Land among the twelve tribes."

So Ahab slouches home and crawls in bed. "Nothing ever works out for me," he pouts, turning his face to the wall and refusing to eat his dinner.

Jezebel comes in to see about him. "Aren't you hungry, sweetheart? Tell mama what's wrong."

"It's that farmer," the king replies. "I offered to pay him for his dumb old vineyard, but no! My money's not good enough for him."

Jezebel sits back in amazement. "And you call yourself a king?" She shakes her head. "That's not how kings behave, my dear. I'll show you how to take care of this little matter! Now eat your supper and you'll feel better." And she hurries off to write a letter to the city council of Naboth's hometown: *It has come to my royal attention that a farmer by the name of Naboth has been heard making threats against my royal person and cursing Yahweh. This kind of behavior cannot be countenanced inside my kingdom. I decree that you shall detain this Naboth and hold a solemn fast, at which time his accusers will appear to make formal charges.* Then she signs the letter with Ahab's name and seals it with his signet ring.

The city council, who live in fear and trembling of the queen, know who is behind this scheme. They immediately arrest Naboth and arrange for his trial. Meanwhile, Jezebel hires two criminal types to testify that they heard the unfortunate farmer threaten the king. Also that Naboth spoke of Yahweh in a most disrespectful manner. (Jezebel thinks this last accusation is an inspired touch of irony.)

With the hired witnesses against him, Naboth doesn't stand a chance. As soon as the trial is over, the city council imposes the punishment prescribed for such a crime—death by stoning. Then they send word to Jezebel that her wishes have been carried out.

When Ahab hears that Naboth is dead, he gets out of bed and hurries down to Jezreel. His darling Jezebel has been as good as her word—she's acquired the vineyard for him. (The property of convicted—not to mention executed—felons reverted to the state.) Though he's not anxious to inquire too closely into the circumstances, he is eager to take possession of the dead man's vineyard.

But who should be waiting for him at the garden gate but his old nemesis Elijah. "What are *you* doing here?" Ahab asks in shock. "You're always spoiling everything!"

"The Living God sent me," Elijah responds. "Why else would I risk coming back? The Lord has a message for you. And you're not going to like it. It goes like this: *You've sold out, Ahab. And now you're going to have to pay. Not only you, but your sons. There won't be any of your heirs left to claim your throne when you're gone. You let Jezebel and her gods take over my people. She's not off the hook either. And her death won't be a pretty sight: the dogs will gnaw her bones down by the ravine where they stoned Naboth.*

Now Ahab is really depressed. And Yahweh-prophets continue to dog his footsteps. On the eve of a war against Assyria, one of them predicts this will be Ahab's last battle. Hoping to outsmart this prophecy, the king puts on the uniform of an ordinary soldier, but the disguise doesn't work. Ahab is shot by a stray arrow. When they bring his chariot back to the city to wash it out after the battle, stray curs gather round and lap up Ahab's blood.

Nevertheless, Jezebel still wields power as queen mother in Samaria. During the next eight years she continues to work at stamping out worship of that Living God who gives her nothing but grief. Politically, however, the kingdom is falling apart. Finally, an army captain named Jehu revolts, threatening to take over the country. When the new king tries to negotiate, Jehu replies, "What peace can there be so long as that witch Jezebel prostitutes our women in Astartes temples?" Jehu defeats the king's forces, fittingly enough, in the very field that Jezebel conspired to steal from Naboth.

Back at the palace, the queen hears the news that Jehu has defeated her son's army and is marching toward Samaria. Instead of hiding or trying to escape, Jezebel goes to her room, takes out her cosmetics, and applies her makeup for the last time. Then she fixes her hair elaborately, as if for a state occasion. When she sees Jehu approaching, she leans out the window of her ivory palace and taunts him. "Perhaps you've heard of Zimri, that other peasant upstart who overthrew his master?" she screams down at him. "Well, just remember what happened to him. He didn't last, and neither will you."

Jehu looks up at Jezebel. He sees not only the painted, aging queen, but the shadowy figures of her attendants shrinking in the shadows. "This is your last chance to save yourselves," he calls out to her servants. "If you're on my side, throw Jezebel down and nothing will happen to you."

Immediately, a couple of eunuchs, who no doubt had experienced their share of the queen's imperious cruelty, grab her and heave her out the window. When Jezebel hits the pavement, her blood stains the walls of her ivory palace and even splatters Jehu's horse. He rides right over her mangled body and up to the palace gate.

Later, after a hearty meal inside, he gives orders that the body be taken up and properly buried. "After all," he says, no doubt thinking of his own newly acquired royal status, "she was a princess." But when the servants go out to recover the body, it's too late. The dogs have already devoured the corpse, just as her old enemy Elijah predicted they would. And no one intervened to salvage the body from desecration, a telling sign of how unpopular the queen was among the people.

For three decades, Jezebel had exercised authority in Israel, perhaps even more than her husband Ahab. But she used that power despotically. Neither her religion nor her politics supplied her with any notion of community or a leader's responsibility. Thus her obvious intelligence, talent, and even courage were wasted in the service of cosmic eroticism.

HERODIAS

Matthew 14:1-12; Mark 6:14-30; Luke 3:1-20, 13:31-33, 23:1-12

𝓘f there had been newspapers during New Testament times, they would have mentioned Jesus only briefly. Some member of the Herodian dynasty, however, would have made the headlines almost every day. Lacking newspaper accounts of the period, we rely on historians of the period, particularly the Jewish Josephus, for our information about this power-hungry clan. Their family tree is impossibly complicated, owing to their penchant for marrying one another, yet they constantly plotted against, denounced, and often killed each other with remarkable abandon. Hated at home by the Jews they ruled, they relied on their contacts in Rome to keep them in power.

Julius Caesar was the first Roman emperor to appoint one of their family as governor of Judea. And for the next 150 years, the Herodians managed to stay in the good graces of whomever was in charge in Rome—no small accomplishment in itself.

We're initially introduced to the family by Herod the Great, the first of his line to bear the title "King of the Jews" and the man responsible for the slaughter of the Bethlehem babies in Matthew 2. Such drastic measures were characteristic of his paranoia in later years; indeed, he murdered three of his own sons, suspecting them of plotting a palace coup. Earlier, however, he had been a strong leader, bringing law and order to the region from Judea to Galilee. To placate the Jews, he even rebuilt their temple in Jerusalem, sparing no expense to restore its splendor. His subjects, however, displayed a puzzling lack of gratitude. He never understood why they should resent his rebuilding Samaria and pagan temples as well.

But that wasn't the only thing that offended them. Herod married a total of ten women, one of them a Samaritan. And the passel of children these marriages produced was constantly fighting for a piece of the royal action. When his children weren't fighting, they were marrying one another to consolidate their power bases.

When the old Herod died, he divided his kingdom, leaving Galilee to his son Herod Antipas. Coming to Rome for his investiture, Antipas stayed in the home of his brother Philip, who'd already been written out of his father's will. We don't know if Antipas brought along his wife, an Arabian princess, but we do know that while he was there, he had an affair with Philip's wife, Herodias. Who, as it happens, is also the old Herod's granddaughter and thus Antipas' niece. Incest is nothing new for Herodias, of course, since Philip, her current husband, is her uncle also.

Herodias, knowing that Philip will never rise much higher than a middle-management position in Rome, decides to swap him for his brother Antipas. She persuades her lover to divorce his Arabian princess and marry her, thus exchanging one uncle-husband for another. When the couple return to Galilee, Herodias takes along her daughter by her first marriage.

For a while, Herodias appears to have made a good career move. Antipas has obviously inherited the leadership skills of his father, and while the Galileans don't love him, he keeps the region on an even keel. Also like his father, he enjoys investing in large-scale public building projects. While Jesus is still a teenager, the beautiful new city of Tiberias begins to rise along the shores of the Sea of Galilee, Antipas' tribute to the new emperor in Rome. As carpenters in Nazareth, only about fifteen miles away, Joseph and Jesus may have worked on the project.

Yet despite Antipas' best efforts, the general populace remains unimpressed. Let these Roman minions build as many new cities as they like. As long as the royal couple continue to flout Jewish law, the Jews regard them as Gentile trash. Incestuous idolaters.

When John the Baptist appears, denouncing the nation's moral failings in no uncertain terms, the people mob the banks of the Jordan, feeling the need to wash away the impurity that contaminates them individually and collectively. They particularly enjoy John's preaching when he accuses government officials of extortion and law officers of police brutality.

Even the Jerusalem bigwigs, the Pharisees and Sadducees, are hiking out to the river to hear him. And John's not afraid to thumb his nose at them either. What kind of leaders are they, anyway? If John were in charge, things would be different. But, of course, one hand washes the other. Those religious fat cats are probably on the take from Herod themselves.

As long as John keeps his operation confined to the wilderness of Judea, Antipas is not overly concerned. After all, that's the jurisdiction of Pontius Pilate, the Roman henchman who's been sent in to take over Judea. In fact, Antipas is even interested in some of John's concepts. But when John moves north, first into Samaria, then into Antipas's own Galilean territory, the tetrarch begins to get nervous. The crowds continue to swell as John's denunciations grow more specific.

"The tetrarch of Galilee, Herod Antipas," John accuses, "is living in sin with his brother's wife. This incest business has got to stop. It's an abomination before the Lord!"

The people love it. Here at last is a spokesman, a prophet,

unafraid to voice publicly their private revulsion at the incestuous and adulterous liaison of Antipas and Herodias. (Note
that, though the marriage is doubly incestuous by dint of marriage between in-laws and between an uncle and his niece,
John calls attention only to the former relationship, forbidden in Leviticus.)[1]

When word of John's attack reaches Herodias, she is furious. He can't call her names and get away with it! She wants
this lunatic the Jews are calling a prophet strung up. That's
the only way to put an end to his ravings.

Antipas is unconcerned about his reputation in Jewish
society, but he is worried about political repercussions. He
hasn't gotten where he is today by pussyfooting with prophets.
John's raving could lead to riots, even foment revolution.
So he decides to put his foot down. The tetrarch has John
arrested and put in prison, which solves two problems. It
should cool the ardor of the reform fanatics John has stirred
up, plus it will keep the man out of Herodias' clutches. Antipas
has no illusions about what will happen should the prophet
fall into his wife's hands.

"Forget John," he probably told Herodias. "I've taken care
of it. He'll never see the light of day again."

But Herodias can't forget. She's been publicly humiliated
by this mangy madman, and she intends to make him pay.

She bides her time until the big birthday bash Antipas
throws every year for his staff. Offering to handle the enter-
tainment, she plans for her daughter—Josephus tells us her
name is Salome—to be the main attraction of the evening.
The girl is a nubile teenager by now, and Herodias is quite
aware of how her dancing will affect her middle-aged stepfather. "Now look, Salome," she tells the girl, "Daddy will just
go crazy when you dance. He'll probably want to give you a
prize. You know how he likes to show off in front of his staff.
So don't just ask for the first thing that pops into your head.
Come and ask me and I'll help you decide."

The plan works easily enough. The men are all carousing

at the stag party. Herodias is waiting in the wings. The music starts. The mother shoves her daughter on stage. It's show time for Salome. And the crowd goes wild.

When the music stops, everyone applauds enthusiastically. Antipas is beaming. As the girl takes her final bow, he holds up his hand. "Wait! Such a performance deserves a reward. What would you like, darling? Just name it—it's yours."

But instead of answering immediately, she runs shyly from the banquet hall to where her mother is waiting backstage. "What should I say?" she asks. "He wants to know what I want. He said anything."

"Wonderful, sweetheart. I have a great idea." And she whispers in her daughter's ear. Maybe Salome wrinkled up her nose in disgust, but Mom seems to want this an awful lot. And it's usually best to let Mom have her way. So Salome returns to the banquet hall.

Her stepfather holds up his hand for silence. "Have you decided what you want? It must be pretty special."

"Oh, it is," Salome says. "And it won't cost much either. The head of John the Baptist on a platter."

Antipas stares at her, his mouth gaping. Then he looks slowly around the banquet hall. All eyes are on him. He knows his guests are holding their collective breath, waiting to see if he'll try to wiggle out of his promise. This is not, he thinks, what he had in mind. He never intended to kill John, just keep him out of harm's way.

He takes a deep breath. Well, he *is* a Herod, and he didn't get where he is today by showing weakness. "Fine, my pet. And you shall have it too. Guard!" And he gives the fateful order for John's execution.

The crowd relaxes. Herod Antipas hasn't lost his edge. He's a chip off the old block, in fact. When the guards return from the prison with the gruesome dessert, Herod has them hand the platter to the girl. And she hurries out to take it to her mother, the only one to look on the gory sight with a smile of pleasure.

Who knows what Antipas and Herodias said to one another that night after the guests had gone home. Perhaps there were mutual recriminations.

"How could you ask such a thing? You know what a following John has. There's sure to be trouble now."

"Well, if you hadn't been so besotted by Salome's little fandango, you would never have made such a dangerous promise. Besides, where's your backbone? Have you lost your nerve? Are you afraid of a few crazy Jews?"

We never see Herodias again in the New Testament account, and Herod Antipas only reappears when Pilate sends Jesus to him at his trial. Whatever stirrings of spiritual interest Antipas may have felt earlier have died away by then, and the tetrarch and his soldiers merely mock the Messiah.

But ancient historians fill in a few final details about the fate of this couple. Antipas' former father-in-law, the Arabian king, undermines the tetrarch's military forces with guerrilla warfare, until Antipas is forced to surrender part of his territory. Public sentiment for John the Baptist remains so strong even years later that the Jews considered this defeat divine retribution for ordering the prophet's death.

In a final blow, Herodias' brother Agrippa, a close friend of the new emperor Caligula, denounces the couple as conspirators. Caligula banishes the tetrarch to the frontier region of Gaul—the Roman equivalent of Siberia. As a favor to his friend Agrippa, Caligula exempts his sister Herodias from the decree. Nevertheless, she follows her husband into exile where they both eventually die. Perhaps she was wise enough to realize that life was never very certain in the court of the mad Caligula.

Like Jezebel centuries before, her use of power was peremptory, based on personal whim. Neither woman had any concept of law, that ideal that transcends individual caprice and thus protects the lowly as well as the highborn. Both women had to resort to trickery to get what they wanted—which in the end, turned out not to be worth the cost.

Business Women

The history of civilization has been swept along on two strong currents. One is war, the other is trade. Commerce both concentrates and disperses populations. Whether in Greek agoras or modern shopping malls, people congregate wherever there's something to buy. When trade routes open, curious travelers venture out to explore the world. In our own time tourists are already pushing back the crumpled Iron Curtain to take a look around.

It is no accident that God planted the Israelites in Palestine, the only land bridge connecting the three continents of Europe, Asia, and Africa. Though never a center of great wealth itself, Palestine was crisscrossed with trade routes, thus fertilizing the rest of the Western world with knowledge of God. From this base the Apostle Paul set out to spread the gospel along roads built, repaired, and protected by the Romans for business purposes.

Rahab, in Canaanite Jericho, sold her most obvious product—her body. But she also appears to have supplemented her earning with weaving. The "virtuous" woman described in Proverbs is a working mother. She deals in real estate and both produces and markets her goods, fine linen cloth.

The "new woman" of the Roman Empire was a major business force. Lydia, Paul's first convert in Europe, is a good example. She was involved in the fabric trade, her specialty being purple dye. She sets up shop in Philippi, the capital of Macedonia, and becomes such a leader in her community that she organizes the group of Gentiles there who retreat to the river on the Sabbath to pray to the Jewish God. As head of her household, which may have included the workers in her shop, she invites the itinerant preacher and his friends to stay in her home, probably because her successful business allowed for such hospitality.

Nowhere in the Bible is there any prohibition against women, whether married or single, mothers or childless, working outside the home. Both in the Old and New Testaments it appears to be the norm. In fact, the early Church owed much of its growth and development to such businesswomen.

RAHAB
Joshua 2; 6; see also Hebrews 11:31; James 2:25

*A*rchaeologists, digging through layers of humanity's oldest known walled city, find evidence that Jericho was repaired or rebuilt at least sixteen times between 3100 and 2100 BC. Why were its citizens so determined to hold on to it? Because the fortress defended an important water source in that arid region, a spring that still irrigates gardens in the Jordan Valley. Also, major trade routes intersected at Jericho since caravans could count on finding water there for their camels.

To the twelve tribes of Israel, finally leaving the desert behind after generations of wandering the desolate Arabian peninsula, Jericho is the gateway to the Promised Land. The only walled city at the southern end of the Jordan River, it also presents their first challenge in Canaan. As any good military strategist would, Joshua, Israel's commander, sends spies ahead of the army to reconnoiter the territory.

The two men see the stone-and-mud walls of the city rising from the plain where spring crops are growing. As they pass through the city gates, they notice the jumble of dwellings

198

and businesses crammed right up to the walls. The noise and crowds overwhelm their senses, more accustomed to the space and freedom of the nomadic life. When night falls, in order to have an escape route handy they look for lodging as close to the walls as possible. They find the perfect place—a brothel right on top of the wall, run by a woman named Rahab.

Prostitution, as a business enterprise, operated differently in Canaan than it does nowadays. Not only was it legal, it was as essential to Middle Eastern agricultural societies as the chemical-fertilizer industry is to ours. The people relied on fertility rites to assure the fruitfulness of their crops, and thus their survival. Both the Jewish law codes and the prophets warned against participating in these fertility rites, using language that clearly indicates they involved ritual sex. Unfortunately, these scriptural passages have generally been taken as only metaphors.

In both the Old Testament and ancient Canaanite scriptures appears the term *qedesha*, a feminine form of the Hebrew root meaning "holy." For Canaanites, the word designated women who engaged in ritual sex. The same term in Israel's law codes, however, means "harlot" or "prostitute." Leviticus warns, "Do not prostitute thy daughter, to cause her to be a whore,"[1] and Deuteronomy commands, "There shall be no whore of the daughters of Israel."[2] Such prohibitions would be necessary only if young women found the business alluring or if it were enticingly lucrative. Perhaps both.

Nevertheless, the book of Joshua records Rahab's occupation straightforwardly, as if recognizing that within her own society she is a respectable businesswoman. By allowing her body to be used for ritual sex, Rahab not only performs a public service but supports her extended family, including her father and mother, sisters and brothers. (No mention is made of either a husband or children.)

Did she also provide "recreational sex" for a price? From a distance of several thousand years it's difficult to know whether such a distinction would have made sense in the

Canaanite culture, anymore than our own church-state dichotomy would mean anything to the Israelites.

At any rate, Rahab's establishment, like the town saloon in the old West, was the logical place for two men from the country to visit when they came to the big city. However, the presence of two strange Israelites has not gone unremarked by the police. When they report them to the king, he orders an immediate search for the two spies. All Jericho has heard of the Israelites' escape from Egypt and their victory over the Amorite kings. Jericho's ruler has no intention of his being the next city state to fall to them.

When the police track the strangers to Rahab's establishment, the king sends her a message: "Hand over the men who are in your brothel. They're spies looking for military information." The fact that the king does not simply send in a SWAT team and capture the men shows that her business operates under a certain amount of protection. Also, the king no doubt is counting on Rahab's patriotism—as well as her cleverness—in capturing the strangers.

But Rahab is already one step ahead of him. Anticipating the arrival of the policemen, she has taken the two men up to her rooftop where she has been "retting" flax, a process that loosens the linen fibers from the stalks by drying them in the sun after the dew has wet them. From time to time the stalks are beaten, which further separates the fibers. Whether Rahab was also a weaver by trade, or a linen merchant, or merely wove linen for her own family's use, we don't know. What we do know is that the flayed stalks of flax made a thatchlike matting, perfect for concealing two grown men.

When the police appear with their summons, Rahab has her story ready. "Gee, you're too late," she says, feigning regret. "They showed up here all right, and I provided the usual services. But I had no idea where they were from. When it began to get dark—just before the city gates shut—they suddenly up and left. Where they went I don't know. But if you hurry, I'm sure you can catch them. They haven't been gone long."

Of course she knows that the search party will head east, in the direction of the Israelite camp. As soon as she hears the city gates swing shut behind them, she hurries up to the rooftop. "You can come out," she whispers to the two spies, "they're gone. Now's the time to make your escape."

The spies creep out from under the mat of flax stalks. "How are we going to get out of here?"

"I can let you down on a rope from my window in the wall," Rahab says. "Once you're safely outside, head west to the mountains. I've sent the police in the opposite direction. Stay holed up in the mountains for three days. That'll give them time to give up the search and come back to the city. That way, you won't blunder into them."

But Rahab has something else to say to the two spies as they're preparing to leave. "Look. I can see which way the wind's blowing. You people can't be stopped. We've heard how your God dried up the Red Sea so you could pass over and escape from the Egyptians. You've already conquered the territory east of the Jordan. We may as well give up. It's obvious that your God's in control—not just of the heavens but the earth as well."

Such an affirmation on Rahab's part amounts to a renunciation of her former religious beliefs. It is not Baal nor his consort Astarte who are responsible for the earth's fertility, but the Living God of the Israelites. The way he's saved those nomads from their better organized and more powerful enemies confirms her belief that he governs all creation.

She also sees, however, that these theological convictions have practical consequences. The Israelites will, inevitably, attack Jericho. And she knows the rules of engagement in Middle Eastern warfare. If the Israelites attack Jericho, she and her family will most likely be slaughtered along with the rest of the city. "Please," she says before she ties the rope to let them down from her window, "swear to me by your Living God that you won't forget what I've done for you. When your army attacks, spare me and my family."

The two spies recognize the fairness of her request. After all, she's saved their lives. But how can they return the favor? They know what warfare is like themselves—wholesale slaughter. "Okay. This is how we'll do it," they tell her. "Tie a red ribbon on your window here. That way we can distinguish it from all the others along the wall. Then, when the siege begins, bring all your family into your house. We can't answer for anyone who ventures outside the confines of your own dwelling. But those who stay indoors will be safe. Deal?"

"Deal," Rahab responds with relief.

But the men hesitate. Being spies, they know they can't afford to take anything for granted here, least of all a foreign prostitute's word. "But remember," they add, "you breathe a word of this to anyone and you're dead meat. Got it?"

"Don't worry," Rahab assures them. "After all, I have a family to think of."

Then she fastens the rope to her window and watches as they disappear into the darkness below. As soon as they're gone she hunts up a strip of linen she's dyed red and hangs it in the same window.

Days go by, filled with anxious waiting. Then one morning she hears a flurry in the streets, people shouting, "The Israelites are coming!" The city gates are shut. Rahab summons all the scattered members of her family to come home quickly. They shut themselves up in the house on top of the wall where they have a good view of all that's taking place outside.

What they see is a most unlikely army. Spread out on the plain below in every direction are encampments. Each family obviously carrying everything they own. Ringing the city walls are men armed with crude weapons, mostly stone axes, clubs, and spears, though some carry sickle-shaped swords. No horses, no chariots. All the soldiers are on foot, marching. But strangest of all is the procession that follows them. Seven men, making a terrible racket with rams' horn trumpets. At the tail end of the parade come a contingent carrying what appears to be a large box on a litter. After marching once around the city walls, the procession disbands. Silence falls outside.

The citizens of Jericho have no idea what to make of these strange goings-on. No doubt appeals are made to the war god during this period, and since Canaanite religion perceived their war god to be in opposition to Baal, the fertility god, Rahab's services are not in demand. Did she begin to wonder if perhaps she'd thrown in her lot with a bunch of lunatics? Well, she probably figures at this point, she has little to lose by keeping the strip of scarlet hanging in her window.

The bizarre processions go on for six days. But on the seventh day, something different happens. The march around the city walls begins earlier than usual—about dawn, in fact. And it keeps up all day. Once, twice, seven times. Finally the parade comes to a halt. The trumpets blast their cacophonous noise. Then all falls silent. Down below, from the motionless soldiers clear to the crowds on the surrounding plain, not a sound is heard. At last a single voice shouts a command and from the distant encampments of Israelites comes an answering roar. The noise swells and rolls across the plain, reverberating against the walls of the city—a sound to send chills up your back.

The walls of the city begin to vibrate, just a little at first, then more dangerously. Mortar starts to crumble; whole stones are dislodged. In moments, entire sections of the fortress are hurtling to the ground, crushing the terrified inhabitants of Jericho beneath them.

From the window Rahab and her family can see it all. Outside they can hear the screams of people being killed, not just by falling debris now but by the Israelite soldiers who are swarming in through the widening breaches in the walls. Their instincts would say *run, leap from the window, if nothing else.* But Rahab keeps order within her house. No one leaves, she says. This is their only hope of survival.

At last, after hours of terror, it's all over. Only one section of the wall remains standing—the few yards supporting Rahab's brothel. As the dust settles, Joshua, the Israelite commander, sends for the two men who served as spies. "Climb up there and bring out the prostitute and her people," he tells them. "Tell them they'll be safe now."

It's instructive to note that when Rahab made the deal with the spies, she bargained not merely for her own life but for those of her family as well. She did not act as an isolated individual, concerned merely for her own skin. Just as she has been her family's chief breadwinner, she took on the responsibility for their rescue as well. She manages to preserve them from the general slaughter.

But what's she to do now? Not only has she lost her city but her business to boot. How is she to support this family now that she must live among these strangers? Prostitution, though not unknown to the men of Israel, is not a respectable trade among them. Joshua does not allow her house to be pillaged, so Rahab's possessions are salvaged. Thus she has something with which to start over. Did she rely on her skill as a weaver to support her family? Did she receive a pension?

The Scripture implies obliquely that Rahab, whatever her other enterprises and despite her former occupation, found a husband among her adopted people. It records that Rahab "dwelleth in Israel even unto this day,"[3] by which we are to understand that she lived on in her descendants. Among those offspring, according to the genealogy listed in Matthew, were Boaz, the husband of Ruth, and eventually David, king of Israel.

And when Joseph, an even later descendant, married a pregnant girl from Nazareth named Mary, he was following in the tradition of his forebear Rahab, erasing the stigma of an outcast woman.

SAPPHIRA

Acts 4:31–5:11; see also Acts 2:42-47

*A*ccounts of the fledgling church in Jerusalem during its first heady days and weeks have always inspired Christians, especially those of us becalmed in the doldrums of affluence. Prosperity buffers both our society and our churches from the thumps and bruises befalling most of the world's population. But prosperity also puts a barrier between us and the kind of living-on-the-edge elation that ignited the early church.

Lest we think that this risky life was an easy choice for those first Christians who had little to lose anyway, the Bible supplies us with the story of Sapphira and her husband, Ananias. In order to understand their story, however, we need to look at the post-Pentecost living arrangements of the Jerusalem church.

Peter, having overcome the cowardice he displayed when he denied knowing Jesus after his arrest, is becoming a powerful preacher, and he and John, his old fishing buddy and sometime rival, are performing miracles of healing. Even being jailed and threatened by the authorities does not dampen their boldness.

This daring of these leaders infects all the new believers, now numbering in the thousands. Their inspiration welds them into a body acting with a single will. Barriers of class and origin suddenly dissolve before the rushing tide of the Holy Spirit. Peter and John, for instance, are perceived as "unlearned and ignorant"[1] by the council of priests and elders examining them. We know they have abandoned their occupation and family connections, which leaves them virtually penniless. In fact, their poverty is emphasized when they stumble across a beggar at the temple. "Silver and gold have I none," Peter tells him, "but such as I have give I thee."[2] Then he takes the beggar's hand, helps him to his feet, and heals him by invoking the name of Jesus.

But impoverished or not, the apostles are the acknowledged leaders of this new community. Meanwhile, members who are landowners or householders don't hesitate to sell those assets and turn the profits over to the apostles in order to provide for the entire body.

People who have never experienced this kind of reckless joy may find such intemperate behavior difficult to credit. Yet it occurs periodically, if not frequently, in human history. Sometimes the results are good, sometimes disastrous. The Plymouth Colony of pilgrims operated in much the same mode, as have any number of religious groups in this country. And in the 1960s and 1970s, bands of hippies all over America, sometimes in cities, more often in rural settings, experimented with communal living. A group called Jesus People USA still live this way in Chicago, sharing their income and expenses.

From the description of the early church that closes the second chapter of Acts, it appears that the people gave up their day jobs to spend most of their time together, either at the temple reveling in their newfound faith or listening to the apostles tell them about this Messiah who had been raised from the dead. When they got hungry, they went to a fellow member's house and ate together. Simple as that. There seemed to be little point in holding onto their money. What good would Roman currency do anyway when Jesus descended from the clouds again, bringing his legions of angels with him this time?

But the early Christians in Jerusalem were not the only communal group in Palestine at the time. Nor were they the only ones awaiting the arrival of a new world order. South of Jerusalem, down along the western coast of the Dead Sea, in the most unlikely spot for a self-sustaining community, lived the Essenes, a monastic community of Jews, mentioned by both Jewish and Greek historians. We know them today as the scribes of the Dead Sea Scrolls, hidden for centuries in caves pocking the bleached cliffs. To preserve the purity of their religion from the corrupting influences of religious and regional politics, the Essenes had withdrawn about 175 BC to this barren stronghold as a sign of their belief that God would one day turn it into a new Garden of Eden when he vindicated those Jews who remained truly faithful. Like John the Baptist, they saw themselves as "preparing a way in the wilderness" for the advent of the Messiah.

Neither ignorant nor uneducated, they had communal living down to a science. Whereas the harum-scarum fellowship of Jerusalem Christians lived hand to mouth on the voluntary contributions of its members, the Essenes had written rules and regulations—and severe penalties for breaking them. One of the Dead Sea Scrolls, "The Community Rule," set forth the mandates for membership, among which was one requiring new members to "bring all their knowledge, their abilities, and their wealth into the community of God, that they may purify their knowledge in the truth of the statutes of God, and may order their abilities according to his perfect ways and all their wealth according to his righteous counsel."[3] An "overseer" administered the funds of their common treasury. For their daily life, the scroll prescribes: "Together they shall eat, together they shall pray, and together they shall take counsel."[4]

Unlike the new Christian community, however, the Essenes were strictly stratified by rank. Refusing to recognize a member's superior rank was a major offense. The Essenes lacked the democratizing tendency of the early church that welcomed all comers, regardless of social status, physical infirmity, national origin, occupation, or gender.

Among the Jerusalem community of new believers is a man called Joseph, a Jew from Cyprus, obviously one of its wealthier members. He owns a parcel of land that he sells, then brings the proceeds and lays the money at the feet of the apostles. For this act of generosity, they call him "Son of Encouragement."

Perhaps it was this public recognition of an outlander that prompts Ananias and Sapphira to dream up their scheme. Whatever their motivation, the Bible makes clear that they are in this together. Like the Cypriot, they own some property, which the story emphasizes they jointly decide to sell. But they also mutually agree to keep back a portion of the proceeds. Perhaps they received more for their land than the Cypriot did and thus can match the amount of his gift and still have some left over for themselves. So they bring the sum they've agreed on and lay it at the apostles' feet, pretending that, like Joseph's, their gift represents the entire sum they received. After all, who wants to be runner-up in this giving game? Thus Sapphira is partner with her husband both in the sale of property and in the deception.

Peter, however, smells something fishy. Keeping secrets is difficult in such a tight-knit community. When he discovers that the pair have misrepresented their actions, as the community's leader he must confront them about their deceit. Otherwise, the spirit of this emerging community will be compromised.

"Ananias," he asks the man, "how could you do such a thing? Lying to the Holy Spirit like that? Did Satan put you up to it? The property was yours to do with as you liked. No one forced you to sell it or make a contribution. And even after you sold it, you were under no obligation to donate the proceeds. How could you even dream that you could get away with such a lie? It's not me you've tried to deceive or even the rest of the community, but God."

When Ananias hears their scheme exposed in this way, he's overcome—whether by shame or remorse we don't know. All we see is the result: he keels over dead. Had he been an Essene, Ananias would also have been ritually cursed and cast out of the community. But Peter utters no such malediction against this fallen brother. What happens instead is that some young men of the community wind the body in a shroud, carry it out, and give it a decent burial.

That's not the end of the story, however. Later in the day Sapphira returns to the community's gathering place, probably a private home. No one has told her of her husband's untimely death.

"Sapphira," Peter says, "tell me again how much you sold that land for?"

Without hesitation, she repeats the same false figure the couple had earlier agreed on.

"How could you two conspire to do such a thing?" Peter responds. "Didn't you know who you were dealing with—trying to trick the very Spirit of God? You hear those footsteps in the hall? That's the young men coming back from the cemetery where they've just buried your husband. Now they've come for you."

Sapphira collapses. The young men come in, find her dead also, and take her body out to bury beside her husband. Partners in business, partners in crime, partners in death.

This strikes us, just as we are told it did the members of that community, as a terrible story. Their original joy was chilled by the fear this event engendered. The couple is stricken, not by Peter, but by their own guilt.

But in a backhanded way, this incident makes a positive point about women. It confirms that they are indeed responsible as individuals for their conduct. As a partner in this business venture, Sapphira is held to the same standards of accountability as her husband. Neither she nor Ananias are allowed to point the finger of blame at the other as Adam and Eve did. In fact, Ananias never speaks at all, only Sapphira. Each is given an equal chance to confess the deception individually. And their individual failures bring the same results. Sapphira is not let off the hook by being portrayed as the victim of her husband's scheming. If nothing else, this story made clear to women in the early church as well as to us that they—and we—are responsible for our own moral choices. In fact, immediately following this tale of deception, Luke's record emphasizes for the first time that "multitudes *both of men and women*"[5] became believers.

PRISCA

Acts 18, Romans 16:3, 1 Corinthians 16:19, 2 Timothy 4:19

For Jews living outside Palestine, existence was always precarious. Scattered over three continents as political exiles, for centuries they nevertheless managed to maintain their religious and ethnic identity wherever they happened to land. For those residing in Rome, however, life was especially unpredictable. Worship of the emperor, a patriotic requirement, put both Jews and Christians at a distinct disadvantage.

When the mad Caligula's reign of terror ended with his assassination, no one expected his handicapped uncle Claudius to run the empire very effectively. Nevertheless, for the next thirteen years Claudius did a creditable job of restabilizing the imperial city. Which included ending the constant ruckuses between the city's Jews and the Jewish Christians (an indication that the gospel had spread quickly to the capital). According to Roman historians, in 49 Claudius settled the matter by simply banishing the lot of them from the imperial city.

Among those forced into exile by this edict were Prisca and her husband, Aquila. (Luke, the author of Acts, the earliest

211

church historian, uses the diminutive form of the woman's name—Priscilla—but the Apostle Paul, who knew her personally, always calls her Prisca in his letters.) Her husband was a Jew born in Asia Minor, but her own national origin is not mentioned. She may have married Aquila before the couple moved to Rome, or she may have been a Roman citizen who met and married him in the capital. They are always named as a pair, and because she is most often mentioned before her husband, an uncommon practice in those times, she may have held higher social rank than Aquila. On the other hand, her personal attainments may have been so impressive that by naming her first both Luke and Paul acknowledge the decisive part she played in the spread of the gospel.

Undeniably, Prisca was a woman of many parts. She was certainly educated. She traveled, she entertained, and with her husband she ran a business, one reported in Acts as tentmaking. Since tents were made of leather as well as goat hair, the term by that time had come to mean leather-worker as well, or even saddler. In any case, after their banishment from Rome, the couple are now plying their trade in Corinth.

Their choice of city shows both an adventurous spirit and entrepreneurial acumen. Uniquely situated on an isthmus, Corinth boasts two ports through which flow most of the Mediterranean goods headed for Europe. Business is booming there. But it's almost carnival-like in its cultural and moral diversity. The term "Corinthian girl" was a byword for prostitute throughout the empire. As for ethnic integrity, only the most aggressively chauvinistic could maintain their cultural boundaries.

Prisca and her husband have already arrived and set up shop in the city a year or more before Paul shows up. Probably they had been members of the Christian faction in their synagogue at Rome, since neither Luke nor Paul mentions their conversion.

When Paul reaches Corinth, he has just suffered a string of disheartening defeats. His visit to Thessalonica ended with his host having to put up bail for him so he can escape his enemies in that city. Moving on to Berea where he at last has some success, his Thessalonian enemies soon follow him there and denounce him as a troublemaker. So he travels to Athens where he has a brief fling with the intellectuals of that city. But after his appearance in the Areopagus—the Athenian equivalent of our television talk shows—Paul's novelty fades and his audience grows bored.

Thus he arrives in Corinth licking his wounds. And no doubt in need of funds. His first item of business is finding a job, which means wandering through the city's marketplace, or agora, and locating a shop where he can hire on, using a skill he's been trained in. In the agora he comes across the stall of Aquila and Prisca and, recognizing them as fellow Jews, applies for a job with them.

This proves to be a providential encounter, not just for Paul but for the emerging Christian church as well. The couple not only furnish him employment, but take Paul into their home. Also, they would introduce him around at the synagogue—which archaeologists have uncovered near the gateway to the agora. On the Sabbath the three of them would attend, Paul, as usual, entering into the discussions of Jewish scripture.

He hesitates to reveal his agenda too quickly this time though, waiting till his traveling companions, Silas and Timothy, arrive from Thessalonica. Then he begins to preach in the synagogue that the Messiah on whom all Jews pin their hopes has already appeared, the one called Jesus.

His message is not welcomed by many members. Once more matters quickly reach a crisis. In his usual fiery way, Paul reacts angrily to the forces opposing him in the synagogue. Finally he denounces them. "I'm not fooling with you hardheaded Jews anymore. From now on, I'm speaking strictly to Gentiles." Then, as if to thumb his nose at them, he moves his preaching operation next door, to the house of a member sympathetic to his cause.

Though some scholars think that at this point, Paul may have begun to teach the Christian message full-time, giving up his work in Prisca and Aquila's shop, such a move seems unlikely. For one thing, Paul frequently points out in his letters that he's not a freeloader, that wherever he goes he always supports himself. For another, the Roman couple's marketplace stall is handy to the house where Paul now does his preaching and provides a perfect public forum for spreading the gospel.

In fact, during the next year and a half the three friends grow closer. Prisca and her husband undoubtedly stand by their obstreperous employee when the orthodox members of the synagogue finally take him to court, bringing against him the usual charges of heresy. When the Roman proconsul in Corinth throws the case out, all three probably breathed a sigh of relief.

Nevertheless, they can see the handwriting on the wall. Prisca and her husband have already been forced to leave one city because of ill will between Jews and Christians. The couple's business is no doubt falling off because of their friendship with Paul. Perhaps they too have become targets for attacks. Or maybe they sense a calling as missionaries themselves. At any rate, the three friends make plans to leave Corinth together.

They sail east, across the Aegean Sea, landing at Ephesus, the capital of Rome's Asian province. From there Paul decides to return to Jerusalem, but Prisca and Aquila settle in Ephesus and unpack their tools and equipment, setting up shop once again in a strange city.

They haven't been there long when yet another flamboyant Jew enters their life, an eloquent rabbi named Apollos. He hails from Alexandria, a renowned intellectual center on the northern coast of Egypt, famous for synthesizing Greek philosophy with Jewish scripture. Apollos is not only an impressive scholar but a thrilling orator. Like Paul, he speaks in the synagogue—though more effectively. Listening to him, the couple discover he has studied carefully the teachings of Jesus.

Yet his obvious learning and dazzling oratory do not blind Prisca to certain gaps in his understanding of the Christian message. Apollos comes down hard on repentance, for instance—the primary theme of John the Baptist—but he says nothing about the transforming power of the Holy Spirit. She sees that Apollos needs further instruction in the gospel himself if he is to represent it adequately.

The manner in which Prisca and Aquila handle the potentially volatile Apollos situation provides the church in Ephesus with an excellent model for dealing with conflict. Instead of confronting him publicly, they approach him in private. Exercising restraint and respect, they patiently unfold the fullness of life in Christ.

For a woman to undertake the instruction of a scholar so obviously erudite as Apollos shows amazing self-confidence on Prisca's part. Indeed, women were relegated to separate screened areas in synagogues and not allowed to enter the discussions that followed the scripture reading. They were not even allowed to touch the Torah scrolls.

No doubt this explains why the couple organized a house-church during their years in Ephesus, a place where women and men together shared in worship. Christianity, a religion that claimed men and women were equal in God's sight, was proving particularly attractive to both Jewish and Gentile women. Indeed, these young churches were dependent on their skills. Thus Prisca suddenly finds herself with a new vocation—teaching.

Once Apollos fully understands the extent of the message he so enthusiastically preaches, he leaves Ephesus for Corinth, taking with him a letter of recommendation from the Ephesian church. Most likely Prisca and Aquila composed this letter, since they had been members of the Corinthian fellowship. Apollos enjoys greater success as a persuasive speaker in the Corinthian synagogue than his predecessor

Paul, a victory he owed in large part to the preparatory instruction he received from Prisca and Aquila.

Soon after Apollos's departure, Paul returns to Ephesus. Once again he goes to work, plying his craft in his friends' workshop. But trouble is still dogging this impassioned apostle. He only lasts three months in the Ephesian synagogue before they too throw him out. At this point Paul insists that the other Jewish Christians leave the synagogue as well, assembling instead in a lecture hall rented from a local teacher. Once Paul is out of their synagogue, the Ephesian Jews seem content to leave him alone.

For a couple of years life remains relatively tranquil for Prisca's household. The church that meets there is thriving. A large part of Paul's ministry now consists of long-distance administration—advising and troubleshooting for the fledgling congregations in Galatia, Philippi, and Corinth via hand-carried letters.

Meanwhile, the Ephesian church, no longer limited to Jews, is growing stronger. Gentiles are giving up their worship of the city's patron goddess, Diana. But the very success of the church brings trouble. The silversmiths of the city are particularly hard hit by a drop in sales of their miniature Diana shrines. They mob a couple of Paul's friends from Macedonia, and soon the entire city is embroiled in a riot. When Paul tries to enter the fray, his friends, very possibly Prisca and Aquila who know his fiery temper, restrain him. Afterward he writes to the church in Rome crediting the couple with saving his life.

Despite his rescue Paul can see that his usefulness in Ephesus is now at an end. He packs his bags, embraces his friends, and leaves the city where he has lived for three years.

Is this the last time Prisca and Aquila ever see their friend? We know they are in Rome when Paul writes to the Christian congregation there during the winter of AD 57–58. The Emperor Claudius had died in 54, opening the door for Jews to return. The couple would have had business affairs in the capital to straighten out after years of exile, and they would also have worked to shore up the reemerging church there.

Their return to Rome is not permanent, however, as we see from Paul's final letter, written to Timothy in AD 67. Paul is himself in Rome then, awaiting death. The apostle mentions many of his former colleagues in this sad missive, but mostly to note their absence or desertion. The only greetings he appends to the letter are to Onesiphorus, an Ephesian who visited him in Rome, and to the ever-loyal Prisca and Aquila.

Prisca makes an enlightening comparison with Sapphira. Both women shared the management of business affairs with their husbands. Both were intimately involved in their churches. But there the similarities end. Sapphira allowed her business to absorb her attention, a choice that ultimately narrowed her life. Prisca, on the other hand, saw her life as whole cloth. She allowed neither the products nor the profit of the small factory she operated to dominate her life. Thus when opportunity arose for her to teach, to counsel, to organize, she was open to those vocations as well. For her, making a living served the larger task of making a life. And because she maintained this larger vision, her work was more than profitable—it was priceless.

Women and the Supernatural

How the Spirit of God works in this world of matter is, as Jesus said, a mystery to us. We can only observe its effects, just as we know the wind is blowing even when we can't see the gusting air itself. The Spirit who hovered over the waters of creation is single and unrivaled; nothing is created by any other source, and no opposite and equal power of evil exists. It is this life-giving Spirit who even now sustains the universe, the invisible power of God animating his creation.

Since the beginning of time, people have sensed, if only dimly, that there is more to this world than meets the eye, that some hidden power lurks behind the visible world. Sometimes out of terror, sometimes in pride, they have tried to tap into this source and harness the energy for their own ends. Sometimes these ends are benevolent, like healing. In other instances, they are evil, like voodoo revenge. Other times they are merely trivial—little more than parlor games.

Regardless of their motive, such quests can be perilous. For one thing, God also manifests his Spirit as fire—"a consuming fire"[1] in the Old Testament, tongues of flame in the New. And playing with fire can be dangerous. But also we may confuse the Spirit of God with other invisible beings he created. Some of these, though outside the range of human vision, are nevertheless like us in their rebellious natures. And just as faithless humans can harm one another, treacherous creatures from this realm can wound and destroy.

Therefore, in order to protect the people from this danger, Israel's law codes forbade dabbling in the incorporeal realm. Deuteronomy 18:10-14 prohibits all exploitation of its energy or intelligence—whether by witchcraft, enchantments, magic spells, or attempts to contact spirits of the dead through necromancy. In the verses that follow this prohibition, God promises to replace such forms of fortunetelling with prophets who will carry his message to the people. However, he makes it clear that he alone must choose the people who will speak for him. And his choices were never restricted by gender. Women prophets named in the Old Testament include Miriam, Deborah, Huldah, Noadiah, and Isaiah's wife. The New Testament adds Anna and the four daughters of Philip the evangelist.

The Old Testament records instances of improper attempts to contact this invisible realm through seers and other sorts of diviners, despite the prohibitions against it. In New Testament times, "unclean" spirits hostile to humanity made frightening incursions into the visible world by "possessing" people's bodies and minds. Then Jesus appears, the Spirit Enfleshed, the only human being with power to control these unruly forces.

THE NECROMANCER OF ENDOR

1 Samuel 28; see also Exodus 22:18, Leviticus 20:27,
Deuteronomy 18:10-22

King Saul has his back to the wall. His kingdom is crumbling, running through his fingers even as he tightens his grasp on it. Internally, his people's confidence in him is ebbing. Externally, the Philistines are eating away his borders. Bouts of madness exhaust his spirit. Even though Jonathan, his heir, still fights by his side, the king knows his son despises him. And just when Saul needs him most, Samuel, the prophet who has always counseled him, deserts him by dying.

Tomorrow Saul knows he must fight what may prove to be his last battle. The Philistines have made deep incursions into northeastern Israel. They are camped at Shunem, within sight of Mount Gilboa, where Saul's troops sit waiting for his orders. Only the Valley of Jezreel lies between the two armies. What will happen to his kingdom if Saul is defeated tomorrow? He already knows the galling answer to that question. That upstart David is waiting in the wings to take over. The kid Saul took under his wing years ago when the boy killed the Philistine giant. For several years now, ever since

Saul chased him off, David has been gathering all the malcontents from Israel for his own army, even hiring out as a
mercenary for Saul's enemies.

The future has never looked so bleak for Saul. What should
he do? Fight or flee? Before he died, Samuel warned him that
the spirit God sent to Saul when he was anointed king had
been recalled. He spoke the truth. Saul has felt its absence for
some time now. When he implores the Lord to speak to him
directly, only silence answers. He's already tried flipping a
coin, rolling dice, even having his dreams analyzed in order
to get some hint of what will happen tomorrow. Nothing. The
prophets he pays to advise him don't come up with anything either. Only Samuel had the kind of access to God Saul
needs now. The future is nothing but a blankness. Worse than
knowing the worst is knowing nothing at all. If only Samuel
were still around.

Then Saul gets a last, desperate idea. Earlier in his career
as king, back when he'd still been God's fair-haired boy, in a
fit of moral earnestness he had issued orders outlawing wiz-
ards and necromancers who conjure up the spirits from the
region of death. That kind of dabbling in the spirit world is
dangerous, Saul knows. But then so are the Philistines. There
must be some medium left in the land somewhere, willing to
come out of retirement this once and arrange a séance with
Samuel. He's the only person, living or dead, that Saul trusts
to tell him the truth about the future.

So the king confers privately with a couple of his trusted
men. "I need a medium," he tells them. "Go find me one."

It doesn't take long. "There's one living in Endor," they
report.

Unfortunately, the town of Endor lies on the far side of
the Philistine army. The trip there will require both courage
and cunning. Saul disguises himself as a common working
man in case they are captured. Then, under cover of night,
he and his men slip out of his tent, down the valley, and
past the enemy encampment. They have to make their way

in the dark over eight miles of rough terrain to the bluff where the town sits. Below, the cliff's walls are pocked with caves. The woman who can conjure spirits from the dead probably lives in one of them.

Though she is often called "the witch of Endor" in later literary references, the woman does not change people into toads or perform magic tricks like witches. She is a "medium," sometimes called a "spiritualist" today. That is, someone who makes her consciousness available to an intermediary spirit, known as her "familiar," who contacts spirits of the dead for her.

The men call out to the woman, and when she appears, she's understandably suspicious of these strangers skulking in the shadows. "I need you to do something for me," one of them says. "I want you to use your powers to call up someone from the Pit. Someone I've got to talk to."

The woman stares at the stranger incredulously. "You've got to be kidding. That kind of thing's against the law. You know what the penalty for conjuring spirits is? I gave that up long ago." She squints at him sharply. "Are you trying to make trouble for me?"

But the stranger persists. "Look," he says, "I've got friends in high places. I swear nothing will happen to you. Just do it, okay?"

So, reluctantly the woman goes about her former business of contacting her "familiar" to communicate with the world of the dead, the place the Hebrews called "the Pit."[1] The Scripture reports the event straightforwardly. Though it provides no details about the paraphernalia and ritual of necromancy, it nevertheless treats the exercise as a reality. And the lady delivers the goods.

"Who do you want to talk to?" the familiar spirit asks, using the medium's voice.

"Call up Samuel," the stranger says.

It is not until the woman sees a figure rising from the ground, a shape no one else can see, that she recognizes the prophet and puts two and two together. She begins to shriek, turning on the stranger. "You're the king, aren't you? Why didn't you tell me? You've tricked me!"

"Don't worry about that," Saul says, brushing aside her anxiety, "just tell me what you see."

"It's like—I don't know—a god rising out of the earth."

"What does he look like? Tell me, tell me," Saul prods her.

"Well, let's see. He's a real old man. And he has on this mantle kind of thing."

Realizing that the prophet, though invisible to him, is amongst them, Saul drops to his knees, bowing his forehead to the ground.

"Why have you troubled me, summoning me from the depths?" demands the ghost of the prophet in a truly sepulchral voice.

"I'm in a terrible mess," Saul cries. "The Philistines are attacking. God has disappeared. He won't talk to me. Not in my dreams, not through my prophets. That's why I've called you up. You've got to help me. Tell me what to do, Samuel. I'm desperate."

And Samuel tells him all right. More than he really wants to know. Tomorrow the Philistines are going to win what will be the final battle for Saul and his sons.

At that news, the king collapses, overcome both by terror and weakness. (He's probably fasted in preparation for the séance.)

Seeing the shape Saul is in, the woman drops her occult role as medium and becomes very practical. "Don't blame me," she tells the prostrate king. "Remember, I only did what you asked me to. I've trusted you with my life. Now if you'll just listen to me, I can at least get you on your feet again. What you need is a good hot meal. Let me fix you something and then you can be on your way."

At first Saul declines. "No, no, I'm fine. Just leave me alone."

But his men agree with the woman. "Come on, chief. We'll

help you to the bed over here where you can rest while she's fixing you a snack."

A snack, indeed, she thinks, and hurries off to kill a calf. While that's roasting, she mixes up some bread dough. There's no time to wait for it to rise. When the midnight repast is ready, she brings it to the men and watches them eat, no doubt amazed at such a turn of events. A king, eating supper in her bedroom!

But by tomorrow night, this man will himself be among those very spirits he commanded her to call up tonight.

Though this woman plays only a bit part in this contest of kings, and we never hear of her again, she is an oddly likable creature. Unlike Shakespeare's witches, she is not depicted as a snaggle-toothed crone who decorates with skulls and cooks with eye of newt. She renounces her occupation as a medium when it is outlawed and only takes it up again under royal pressure. No one even offers to cross her palm with silver during the transaction. And when Saul swoons after his encounter with the underworld, she sensibly, even generously, turns to a practical, physical remedy for his feebleness.

In fact, if Saul, like this woman, had accepted the changing circumstances of life, if he had retired from his former career as gracefully as she did, he would not have felt the need to countermand his own laws. And he might never have had to fight that final disastrous battle.

HULDAH

2 Kings 22, 2 Chronicles 34

*I*n 621 BC Jerusalem was hardly the same city where David once dreamed of building a house for the Lord. The temple his son Solomon had completed three centuries ago still stood atop the hill that dominated the city, but over the years Egyptian armies and Philistine marauders had repeatedly looted it. Now sheer neglect was taking its toll. More popular shrines, dedicated to Baal, Astarte, and Molech, now peppered the landscape. Worship of these gods supported a number of lucrative industries, including metalsmithing, weaving, and cultic prostitution, both male and female. Yahweh, the Invisible, who had no fertility consort and of whom no images were allowed, had lost out to the more exciting competition, gods who gave you something visible, something tangible. And those gods had the added advantage of not interfering with your personal life. Except, of course, when times were really bad and you might have to sacrifice one of your children.

Small wonder then that the temple of Yahweh, once the pride of the city, had fallen into disrepair. The roof leaked; the walls were crumbling. Manasseh, king of Judah for fifty-five years, had effectively squelched the public worship of Yahweh during his reign. After his death, his son Amon had ruled only for two years when he was killed in an unsuccessful palace coup, leaving his eight-year-old son Josiah as king.

Since his father's untimely death, Josiah's mother has played a large part in her son's education and spiritual formation. Perhaps she's the one responsible for opening her son's eyes to Judah's problems. At any rate, in his midteens, the boy king now rules a kingdom politically more secure than it has been in a long time. The constant threat from the Assyrian Empire is waning. Yet Josiah sees that something is drastically wrong with his country, and he senses that the problem springs from the gods his people worship.

Since Judah can now afford to put its resources into something besides defense, Josiah decides to spend the necessary funds to repair the temple. At least it's a start in the right direction.

One day he sends Shaphan, his secretary of state, to the temple to get an accounting of the funds the priests have collected to pay the skilled laborers working on the restoration project. While he's there, Hilkiah, one of the priests, shows Shaphan a scroll recently discovered when the rubble was being cleared away. "Look at this," he says, "it's an amazing discovery—the Book of the Law!"

According to biblical scholars, this lost scroll must have been composed of large chunks of what we now know as Deuteronomy. It contains laws governing everything from how to keep a kosher kitchen to reparations for crime victims. Looking it over, Shaphan agrees with Hilkiah that this is quite a find indeed. He takes it back to the palace and reads it to the king. When he gets to the last section, which describes the disasters that will befall people who fail to follow these laws, Josiah is appalled. His people are observing none of these rules. No wonder they're in such a fix.

Nevertheless, Josiah proceeds cautiously. He can't act

merely out of his own emotional response to this document. What if it's a hoax? Not only does he need some verification of the scroll's authenticity, but he needs to know how he can straighten his country out after it has followed a false path for so many years. So he sends a delegation of government and temple representatives, led by the priest Hilkiah, to "inquire of the Lord"[1] both for himself and on behalf of his people.

"Inquiring of the Lord" is a technical term for obtaining the services of a prophet. And there were a number around, warning the people of exactly the kinds of calamities the scroll predicted. Zephaniah, for one, who happened to be the king's cousin. And Jeremiah had already been prophesying for five years. So why didn't the delegation choose one of them? Probably because neither possessed the expertise necessary to assess the newly discovered document. The delegation needed someone they could trust to speak for the Lord but who also had a scholar's familiarity with the ancient laws, which were even more neglected than the temple. It wouldn't hurt if this person had some understanding of the royal court's interest in this matter as well.

Thus they settle on Huldah, perhaps because she is both a scholar and has suitable court connections. Married to Shallum, keeper of the royal wardrobe, she will understand the need for discretion.

Huldah lives in "the college,"[2] what later translations call "the Second Quarter" of Jerusalem.[3] The Hebrew word, however, is *mishneh*, meaning "place of repetition," since education was primarily an oral affair in the ancient world. We assume, therefore, that Huldah was a teacher in the quarter immediately adjacent to the temple. The deputation from the king probably seeks her out because of her learning and expertise on legal matters. Even Hilkiah, the high priest, is willing to accept her judgment on the authenticity of the recently uncovered scroll. Huldah's part in this story shows that women were sometimes teachers and scholars in Old Testament times.

But even more important, Huldah is a prophetess. The Hebrew word used to describe her calling is the feminine form of the same word identifying the vocation of Isaiah, Jeremiah, and all other Old Testament prophets. Being a prophet was not the same as being a "seer." Prophecy is not a career choice. Natural abilities or training do not prepare one for the task, only a direct call from the Lord. The Old Testament designates several women as prophets, including Miriam, Moses' sister, and Deborah, a judge over Israel during the early years in Palestine. The woman most like Huldah, however, is Anna, a prophetess in the New Testament who also lived within the temple precincts and "served God with fastings and prayers night and day."[4]

As a teacher and scholar, Huldah may have been deliberate and methodical. But as a prophet, she doesn't pussyfoot around. After examining the book of the Law and deciding it is authentic, she delivers the Lord's message for the king, prefacing her remarks with the same formula all prophets of Yahweh used: "Thus saith the Lord." In fact, she inserts these words into her message twice more before she finishes. And unlike some oracular prophecies, there is nothing obscure in what Huldah says.

"Tell the man who sent you to me," she begins, letting the delegation from the palace know with this veiled note of irony that her prophetic powers have already discerned his identity, "that this is what the Lord says: 'Things are every bit as bad as the king of Judah thinks they are. This is one story that's going to come true. The people of this land have forgotten about me and taken up worship of false gods, so let's see if those gods that they make with their own hands can protect them from my anger.'"

No doubt the delegation swallowed hard at that one. They were the ones who had to return to the palace and deliver the bad news to the king. But then Huldah modulates the message a bit.

"However," she adds, this time addressing the message

of the Lord directly to Josiah, "'because I saw how the words of the Law wounded your heart when you heard them and how sincerely you mourned for the judgment that must inevitably befall your land because of the people's unfaithfulness, I'm at least going to show you a little mercy. Go ahead and carry out your reforms; do the best job you can. Though the damage to the nation is irreversible, nevertheless, you'll be spared the sight of your people's suffering. You won't live to see the punishment that waits in the wings for the unrepentant.'"

When Huldah finishes this pronouncement, the group of officials quickly leave her. Doubtless they had heard enough for one day.

Huldah, of course, would know, as all true prophets did, that these prognostications of doom include her. The judgment hanging over Jerusalem will fall, like the rain, on the just as well as the unjust. It took courage to be a prophetess, to open a window to the future when the view was so dark.

MARY MAGDALENE
Matthew 27:55–28:10; Mark 15:40–16:11;
Luke 8:1-3, 23:48–24:11; John 19:25–20:18

*M*agdala, a small village on the Sea of Galilee's western coast, has only one claim to fame. It was home to the woman who came to be called "the Magdalene," probably because she had no family to supply her a surname. Since both Mark and Luke say that Jesus cast seven devils out of her, we can assume she hadn't been the easiest person in the world to live with. She may well have been such a threat to her family that they were forced to bar her from the house. If the Gerasene demoniac's antics are any indication of how people possessed of multiple hostile spirits behave, her family may have had no choice. The Gerasene tore off his clothes, wandered naked among the tombs, and was driven to such violent frenzies that the community had to chain him up. Even that could not always restrain him. He'd been known to break the chains and run howling into the wilderness.

That's the kind of life Mary had before Jesus found her. Strangely enough, despite the fact that she became a member of the new Messiah's entourage, there is no account of their initial encounter. Was no one else present for this exorcism? Surely such a spectacular event would have found its way into at least one of the gospels if either Jesus or Mary had recounted it. The gruesome details remain private, however, no doubt because they would have caused Mary unnecessary humiliation.

Like the Gerasene demoniac—note that he too is identified by a geographical designation rather than a family name—Mary is eager to follow Jesus. But the Healer sends the Gerasene back to his own home as a demonstration of God's power and graciousness, while he takes Mary into the band accompanying him on his preaching tours. Perhaps the Gerasene had a family willing to take him back and Mary didn't. Perhaps the community of Magdala couldn't forget her previous behavior—though we should note that, despite the legends that have grown up around her name, the text contains absolutely no indication that she was either a prostitute or the town tramp.

More likely, she is added to the entourage because she possesses some particular skill or aptitude. Luke records that, in addition to the twelve disciples who accompanied Jesus as he went from town to town preaching, were "certain women, which had been healed of evil spirits and infirmities."[1] Luke mentions in particular Joanna, whose husband was right-hand man to the tetrarch of Galilee, Herod Antipas. Since Luke includes more material about Herod than any of the other gospels, Joanna may well have been Luke's source of information about the ruler. Next comes Susanna, about whom we know nothing more, except that, like the "many others" who are nameless, she uses her own private funds to support this mission.

Thus all these women are mentioned because they have a particular contribution to make. And Mary Magdalene heads the list, with the notation about the seven devils. Like the medium of Endor and the prophets Huldah and Anna, Mary has firsthand experience of what we may call the spirit world, that mysterious invisible realm, charged with power more dangerous than a nuclear reactor.

Though we tend to discount demons in the twentieth century, they show up not only in the Bible but in other ancient documents of world religions, as well as in ancient secular histories and literature. Since the behavior produced by demon-possession looks a good bit like what we now call mental illness, we often explain the former in terms of the latter. Yet we are much too ignorant of either phenomenon to make any ironclad assumptions about their relationship.

Perhaps in reaction against our society's tendency to make the spirit realm seem more manageable by explaining it in medical terminology, two trends have developed recently. One is called, rather vaguely, the New Age movement. Some of its adherents claim they can contact the spirit world, much as the Endor medium did. Others simply look for a private pipeline into the power generated by spiritual sources, mistakenly thinking those sources are as undemanding and controllable as an electrical outlet.

The other trend, though followed largely by Christians, is based on surprisingly similar assumptions. The current fascination with "spiritual warfare" and angels can also be dangerous, especially if the spiritual realm is presumed to be either utterly benign or completely at our disposal. The spirits, as Mary Magdalene knew to her sorrow, possess not only power but will, one not always kindly disposed toward humanity. And its power is both stronger and more clever than most human beings.

Nevertheless, Mary's experience of that shadowy world was important to Jesus' work, a large part of which consisted of calling these hostile forces out of the human bodies they inhabited. We don't know if Mary actually assisted in the exorcism process, but she certainly would have been helpful during the recovery. Who more than she knew what the loss of personality meant, what the violation of one's own spirit felt like?

But her part in the gospels goes far beyond that of assistant exorcist or post-traumatic counselor. Her largest contribution to Jesus' story comes at the climax. Mary Magdalene is named, usually first, in three of the gospels as a witness to the Crucifixion. (Luke mentions "the women that followed him from Galilee,"[2] naming none of them.) She, along with "the other Mary,"[3] probably Jesus' mother, watch as Joseph of Arimathea has the corpse removed from the cross, wrapped in a linen shroud, and carried to his own sepulcher. There, in a rock outcrop not far from the city, he has the body sealed up by rolling the stone door across the mouth of the cavelike tomb.

The two Marys, along with Salome, have to wait till the shops open the next evening after the sun goes down and the Sabbath officially ends before they can slip out to buy the necessary spices and ointments for the body. They bring these back to the house, probably where all the followers of Jesus are hiding, and wait through the night before they can return to the tomb and perform this last service for their kinsman and friend. It seems a meager gesture, a mere token of respect for their dead rabbi's tortured body, but their ministering to Jesus has not ended with his death.

They leave the city before dawn and reach the tomb at daybreak. Along the way they have been fretting over that stone door. It weighs a ton or more. There's no way three women can even budge it. Will there be someone around, a workman with tools perhaps, who can help them? But as they enter the burial grounds, what they see is not the stubborn stone but the gaping dark mouth of the sepulcher.

Mary Magdalene, probably a good bit younger than the two other women who are old enough to be grandmothers, reaches the tomb first. As John remembers the story, the two other women fade into the background altogether. What can this unsealed tomb mean? They step inside to investigate and see—not a corpse in its linen shroud, but a young man sitting on the ledge where the body had lain. Mark, the plainest of the gospels, says he was "dressed all in white."[4] Matthew identifies the young man as an angel, and Luke adds a second man, with "light cascading over them."[5]

Light or no light, this is a fearsome and unexpected sight. What has happened to the body? Has it been stolen?

Then the young man inside the tomb gives them an equally puzzling message. "Jesus—the one from Nazareth, the one recently crucified—he's not here anymore. He is raised up. Remember? He told you it would happen. Now go and tell the others. Jesus is going to Galilee, and he wants you all to meet him there."

Not waiting to question this shining young man further, they stumble out of the tomb, into broad daylight, reeling with implications too enormous to take in at once. Hurrying back to the house in Jerusalem, they report what they have seen at the cemetery and what the young man told them.

What happens next varies rather widely in the gospel accounts. But all four attest that most of the men don't believe the women. Luke reports that Joanna and the other women attempt to convince the men to believe the three women, but "their words seemed to them as idle tales, and they believed them not."[6]

It's obvious to most of the men that these women are badly shaken. Who knows what they really saw? Maybe it was the wrong tomb. Maybe they saw a corpse and it rattled them. They should never have ventured out alone in the first place. All that spice-and-ointment folderol was unnecessary anyway. Besides, everyone knows the Magdalene's background. Hanging around tombs is dangerous for her emotional stability. She's apparently the ringleader and has managed to stir up the other two women. They eye her uneasily. Maybe now that Jesus is dead and can't protect her from the unclean spirits, those seven devils are coming back to haunt her.

According to John, however, Peter and "the other disciple"[7] immediately take off for the tomb, racing one another to be the first one there. They stumble in, confirm that the corpse is missing, and leave.

Mary Magdalene follows them back to the cemetery. After the men return to the city, leaving her there alone, she drops to her knees outside the dark hole, in tears. Maybe she is crying from frustration as well as grief. First the other disciples of Jesus doubt her word, then these two ignore and abandon her. Now it looks as if Jesus himself has absconded. Or has been stolen away.

Just then she looks up and sees two men in white inside the shadowy sepulcher.

"What are you crying for, lady?" they ask.

"It looks as if someone has stolen my Master's body, and I have no idea where to look for him now."

She gets to her feet and, as she turns to go, almost bumps into another man standing behind her. She averts her eyes, hiding her tears from the stranger.

The man speaks to her though. "What's the matter, lady? Why are you crying? Are you looking for someone?"

It's the cemetery attendant, she thinks as she turns away, the one who tends the grounds here. Yet his tone sounds challenging, as if he knows something about all this. "Mister," she says, "if you've put him someplace else, please tell me. If you don't want him here, I'll be glad to take him off your hands."

Then the man speaks only one word—"Mary"—and instantly the world lights up again. She *knows* who this is.

"Rabboni!" she cries, turning toward him. Sinking to her knees once more, she throws her arms around his knees.

Later that same day, his disciples, still hiding out in the upper room, will be afraid of Jesus when he appears there; they take him for a ghost just because he can walk through walls. He has to coax Thomas to touch him, to feel his wounds in order to assure himself that this body, though transformed by resurrection, is nevertheless still flesh and blood. Mary, however, knows the difference between a mere ghost and a living person when she sees one. The torment she suffered under the hostile spirits' domination has sharpened her spiritual perception. Her reaction to Jesus in the garden is not fear but joy.

But now Jesus holds up his hand. "You mustn't cling to me like this," he cautions her. "I'm still going to have to leave you again and return to my Father." Then he continues, "But don't let that trouble you. My Father is also your Father, and my God is your God too. What I want you to do now is go back to my brothers in Jerusalem and tell them what's become of me and where I'm going."

And with that consoling commission, Mary Magdalene gets to her feet once more and returns to the city with her message for his followers. She doesn't care whether they believe her or not. Whether they accept her as Christ's envoy is beside the point. She has been the first person in all the world, in all of history, to recognize the risen Lord, and nothing—not their doubt nor their disdain—can stop her from proclaiming his living presence.

NOTES

EVE
1. Genesis 1:27, KJV.
2. Genesis 5:2, KJV.
3. Genesis 2:8, KJV.
4. Genesis 3:7, KJV.
5. Genesis 3:7, KJV.
6. Genesis 3:16, KJV.
7. Genesis 3:20, KJV.

SARAH
1. Genesis 6:2, KJV.
2. Genesis 6:2, KJV.
3. Genesis 6:4, KJV.
4. Genesis 17:4, KJV.
5. Genesis 21:6-7, RSV.

MARY
1. Luke 1:29, KJV.
2. Matthew 13:55, KJV.
3. John 2:4, KJV.
4. Mark 3:33, RSV.
5. Luke 14:26, KJV.
6. Luke 1:38, KJV.
7. John 19:26, KJV.
8. John 19:27, KJV.

RUTH
1. Ruth 1:29, KJV.
2. Genesis 38. This is not the same Tamar as in 2 Samuel 13.

MICHAL AND ABIGAIL
1. Deuteronomy 21:14, KJV.
2. 2 Samuel 3:16, KJV.

WOMEN ON THE OUTSIDE
1. Acts 1:8, KJV.

HAGAR
1. Genesis 16:3, NIV.

2. Genesis 16:8, NIV.
3. Genesis 16:8, NIV.
4. Genesis 16:13, NIV.

SYRO-PHOENICIAN WOMAN
1. Acts 16:17, NIV.
2. Luke 18:1, RSV.
3. Luke 18:7,8; RSV.

WOMAN WITH THE ISSUE OF BLOOD
1. Mark 5:25, KJV.
2. Leviticus 15:25, NIV.
3. Mark 5:26, KJV.
4. Luke 8:45, NIV.
5. Mark 5:34, KJV.

WOMEN AND VIOLENCE
1. Judges 19:30, KJV.
2. Judges 21:25, KJV.

TAMAR
1. 2 Samuel 13:3, KJV.
2. 2 Samuel 13:4, KJV.

WOMAN TAKEN IN ADULTERY
1. Deuteronomy 18:13, NIV.
2. Deuteronomy 17:7, NIV.
3. John 8:11, RSV.

SENSUAL WOMEN
1. Genesis 2:9, KJV.
2. Genesis 3:6, KJV.

SHULAMMITE MAIDEN
1. Song of Solomon 1:5, KJV.
2. Song of Solomon 1:5, KJV.
3. Song of Solomon 1:6, KJV.
4. Song of Solomon 2:10-13, KJV.
5. Song of Solomon 3:8, KJV.
6. Song of Solomon 4:2, KJV.
7. Song of Solomon 4:16, KJV.
8. Song of Solomon 5:1, KJV.
9. Song of Solomon 5:2, KJV.
10. Song of Solomon 5:3, KJV.
11. Song of Solomon 5:16, KJV.
12. Song of Solomon 7:1, KJV.

13. Song of Solomon 7:5, KJV.
14. Song of Solomon 8:3, KJV, emphasis added.
15. Song of Solomon 2:7, KJV.
16. Song of Solomon 8:4, KJV, note.
17. Song of Solomon 8:13, KJV.

MARY OF BETHANY
 1. Luke 10:42, KJV.

MARTHA
 1. Luke 10:40, NIV.
 2. Luke 10:40, KJV.
 3. Luke 10:41, KJV.
 4. John 11:4, KJV.
 5. John 11:5, KJV.
 6. John 11:11, KJV.
 7. John 11:23, NIV.
 8. John 11:39, KJV.

REBEKAH
 1. Genesis 24:67, NIV.
 2. Genesis 24:67, KJV.
 3. Genesis 25:27, NIV.
 4. Genesis 26:8, KJV.

SALOME
 1. Matthew 27:55-56, KJV.
 2. Matthew 27:56, KJV; see also Mark 15:40, KJV.
 3. Matthew 19:30, KJV.
 4. Matthew 20:16, KJV.

ESTHER
 1. Esther 2:14, KJV.
 2. Esther 4:16, KJV.

JEZEBEL
 1. Judges 21:25, KJV.
 2. *Ba'al* is a Hebrew word meaning "master" or "husband." All
    Palestinian peoples used the term to address their deities,
    including the Israelites. From the time of Ahab on, however,
    it came to signify only the fertility god of the region and
    dropped from Israel's vocabulary of worship. The particular
    form of Ba'al worshiped by Jezebel's father was Melqart.
 3. Prophets of this period lived in communities, somewhat like
    monks of a later age, often under the tutelage of a master
    prophet. People consulted them for direction on matters

requiring difficult decisions, hoping to receive an "oracle" or message from whatever deity the prophets served. The king employed companies of prophets as counselors, often ones who told him only what he wanted to hear.

HERODIAS
1. Leviticus 18:16. The Essene community at Qumran, however, extended its definition of incest to include an uncle–niece liaison.

RAHAB
1. Leviticus 19:29, KJV.
2. Deuteronomy 23:17, KJV.
3. Joshua 6:25, KJV.

SAPPHIRA
1. Acts 4:13, KJV.
2. Acts 3:6, KJV.
3. Michael A. Knibb, *The Qumran Community*, vol. 2 of *Cambridge Commentaries on Writings of the Jewish and Christian World 200 B.C. to A.C. 200* (Cambridge, England: Cambridge University Press, 1987), page 79.
4. Knibb, page 113.
5. Acts 5:14, KJV, emphasis added.

WOMEN AND THE SUPERNATURAL
1. Deuteronomy 4:24, KJV.

THE NECROMANCER OF ENDOR
1. Psalm 103:4, NIV.

HULDAH
1. 2 Kings 22:13, KJV.
2. 2 Kings 22:14, KJV.
3. 2 Kings 22:14, RSV. The NIV uses "Second District."
4. Luke 2:37, KJV.

MARY MAGDALENE
1. Luke 8:2, KJV.
2. Luke 23:49, KJV.
3. Matthew 27:61, KJV.
4. Eugene H. Peterson, *The Message: The New Testament in Contemporary English* (Colorado Springs, CO: NavPress, 1993), page 112.
5. Peterson, page 179.
6. Luke 20:2, KJV.
7. John 20:3, NIV.